CONTENTS

ACT 1

1 A ship carrying King Alonso of Naples, his brother Sebastian, and other members of his court is struck by a storm. The storm is so strong that the ship's crew are not able to prevent the ship from splitting apart.

2 On a nearby island the magician Prospero reassures his daughter, Miranda, that no-one on the ship has been harmed. He tells her that he was once Duke of Milan, but his brother, Antonio, stole his title from him, helped by King Alonso. Prospero created the storm in order to bring Antonio, Alonso, and their companions to the island. Ariel, Prospero's spirit-servant, helped him to create the storm. The spirit does not want to be Prospero's servant any longer, but Prospero saved Ariel from torment by a witch, so the spirit owes a duty to him. Caliban, a strange creature who is the witch's son, angrily curses Prospero for having stolen the island from him. Ariel leads in Ferdinand, the King's son. As Prospero planned, Ferdinand and Miranda quickly fall in love. Prospero, however, wants to make it hard for Ferdinand to win Miranda and so uses his magic to enslave him. Ferdinand accepts this because he is happy as long as he can see Miranda.

Act 2

1 King Alonso, Antonio, Sebastian (Alonso's brother), and others from the ship are now lost on the island. Alonso is devastated because he believes that his son, Ferdinand, is dead and Gonzalo, his advisor, tries to comfort him. Ariel puts a spell on everyone, except Antonio and Sebastian, to make them fall asleep. Antonio persuades Sebastian to murder Alonso so that he will replace him as King of Naples. As Sebastian and Antonio draw their swords to kill the sleeping Alonso and Gonzalo, Ariel causes everyone to wake up. They all depart to try and find Ferdinand.

2 When Caliban sees Trinculo, the King's jester, he hides under his cloak. However, another storm is approaching and Trinculo also gets under Caliban's cloak to shelter from it. Stephano, the butler, arrives and thinks he has found a four-legged monster. Stephano gives the 'monster' some of his strong wine and Caliban begins to worship Stephano as a god. Caliban promises to show them where to find fresh water and food on the island.

ACT 3

1 As Prospero's slave, Ferdinand has to carry logs for him. Miranda feels sorry for Ferdinand, but he is happy to perform this task as long as he can see Miranda. Miranda and Ferdinand declare their love for one another and she offers to marry him. Prospero has been secretly watching them and is very happy that this part of his plan has been successful.

2 While they are exploring the island, Caliban tells Stephano and Trinculo that Prospero is a magician who stole the island from him. He encourages them to kill Prospero and promises to take them to him. Ariel overhears their conversation and goes to warn Prospero.

3 Prospero causes spirits to bring a feast to King Alonso and his companions. However, before they can eat, Ariel appears in the shape of a monster and reminds Alonso, Antonio, and Sebastian of their sins. Alonso feels guilty for helping Antonio to overthrow Prospero. Sebastian and Antonio react differently and run off determined to fight the monsters or devils they think are around them on the island.

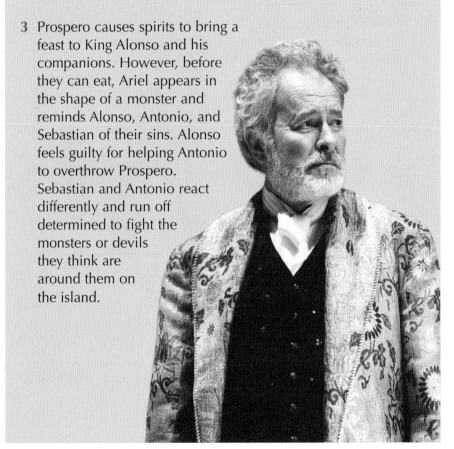

Act 4

1   Prospero agrees to allow Miranda to marry Ferdinand.
    He calls his spirits to perform an entertainment to celebrate
    their love and to bless them. Suddenly, Prospero remembers
    that Caliban, Stephano, and Trinculo are plotting to kill him.
    He tells Ariel to hang some flashy clothing in their way.
    Having been led through bushes and into a stinking pond by
    Ariel, Trinculo and Stephano are distracted by the clothing
    outside Prospero's cave and start trying it on. With Caliban,
    they are chased out by spirits in the shape of hunting dogs.

Act 5

1   Prospero tells Ariel that he will not take further revenge
    on his enemies. He vows to give up his magic once his plan
    is complete. When Alonso and his companions enter, under
    a spell, Prospero addresses them in turn and at last reveals
    who he really is. Alonso asks Prospero to forgive him. When
    Alonso grieves over the loss of his son, Prospero reveals
    Ferdinand and Miranda playing chess. Ariel brings in the
    ship's Master and Boatswain, followed by Caliban, Stephano,
    and Trinculo. Prospero invites Alonso and his companions to
    spend the night at his cave before they all sail home to
    Naples the next day. Finally, Prospero releases Ariel.

Epilogue

Prospero asks the audience to release him from the island by
applauding the play.

FROM THE SHIP

ALONSO
King of Naples
He helped Antonio to
overthrow Prospero

FERDINAND
Alonso's son
He falls in love with Miranda

ANTONIO
Prospero's brother
He stole the Dukedom of Milan
from Prospero. He persuades
Sebastian to try to kill Alonso

SEBASTIAN
Alonso's brother
He plots with Antonio to
kill Alonso

GONZALO
Alonso's old advisor
He helped Prospero when
he was forced out of Milan

ADRIAN AND FRANCISCO
Two lords

STEPHANO
A butler
He plots with Caliban to kill
Prospero

TRINCULO
A jester
He is Stephano's friend and joins
in the plot to kill Prospero

THE BOATSWAIN
*Officer in charge
of the sailors*

THE MASTER OF THE SHIP
The Captain

THE SHIP'S CREW

ON THE ISLAND

PROSPERO
The rightful Duke of Milan
He now uses magic to bring
the passengers from the ship to
his island

MIRANDA
Prospero's daughter
She falls in love with
Ferdinand, King Alonso's son

ARIEL
A spirit who has become
Prospero's servant
Ariel carries out much of
Prospero's magic for him

CALIBAN
A witch's son
He was on the island before
Prospero arrived and is now
Prospero's slave

SPIRITS
Other spirits who act
under Prospero and
Ariel's direction

CHARACTERS IN THE MASQUE, PLAYED BY ARIEL AND OTHER SPIRITS

JUNO
Queen of the gods

IRIS
Goddess of the
rainbow and Juno's
messenger

CERES
Goddess of the harvest
and the earth

Ninagawa Company, 1992

West Yorkshire Playhouse, 1999

Shakespeare's Globe, 2000

Sheffield Crucible, 2002

RSC, 1982

Ninagawa Company, 1992

RSC, 1995

RSC, 1993

RSC, 1988

RSC, 1993

RSC, 1982

Almeida Theatre, 2000

The Tempest, 1979 (directed by D. Jarman)

Sheffield Crucible, 2002

Shakespeare's Globe, 2000

RSC, 1998

RSC, 1993

RSC, 1998

RSC, 1982

West Yorkshire Playhouse, 1999

RSC, 1982

RSC, 1993

Open Air Theatre, Regent's Park, 1996

Almeida Theatre, 2000

ON THE ISLAND

PROSPERO *the rightful Duke of Milan*

MIRANDA *his daughter*

CALIBAN *a savage and deformed slave*

ARIEL *an airy spirit*

SPIRITS *in the service of Prospero who also appear as* IRIS, CERES, JUNO, *Nymphs, Reapers, dogs, etc.*

SHIPWRECKED

ALONSO *King of Naples*

FERDINAND *his son*

SEBASTIAN *Alonso's brother*

ANTONIO *Prospero's brother, usurping Duke of Milan*

GONZALO *an honest old councillor*

ADRIAN
} *lords*
FRANCISCO

STEPHANO *a drunken butler*

TRINCULO *a jester*

MASTER *Captain of the ship*

BOATSWAIN
} *crew of the ship*
MARINERS

Scenes take place on a ship at sea, then on the island.

23

In this scene ...

- A storm has struck the ship carrying King Alonso of Naples, his brother Sebastian, and other members of his court.
- Despite the crew's best efforts to keep the ship afloat, it splits apart.

The ship carrying Alonso, King of Naples, has been hit by a violent storm and the crew are struggling to keep it afloat.

s.d.   **ship's Master**: Ship's captain

s.d.   **Boatswain**: a ship's officer in charge of sailors

2   **What cheer?**: How are things going?

3   **Good**: i.e. it's good that you are here promptly

Fall to it yarely: Get to work quickly

5   **Cheerly**: Get stuck in

6   **Take in the topsail**: i.e. to reduce the ship's speed

Tend to: Pay attention to

8   **if room enough**: as long as the ship has room to manoeuvre

9–10   **Play the men**: Act like men

12   **bosun**: another spelling of boatswain

13   **mar our labour**: i.e. get in the way

16   **Hence**: Go away

16–17   **What ... King?**: These roaring waves aren't impressed by kings

19   **councillor**: close advisor to the King

20–1   **work ... present**: calm things down now

Think about

- If you were the director, how would you create this opening scene of a ship in a storm at sea? Think about sound effects, the set and characters' movements.

- What effect do you think this opening scene might have on a theatre audience?

24

On a ship at sea. A storm with thunder and lightning.

Enter a ship's Master *and a* Boatswain.

Master	Boatswain!
Boatswain	Here, Master. What cheer?
Master	Good. Speak to the mariners. Fall to it yarely, or we run ourselves aground! Bestir, bestir!

Exit.

Enter Mariners.

Boatswain	Heigh, my hearts! Cheerly, cheerly, my hearts! Yare, yare! Take in the topsail. Tend to the Master's whistle. (*Shouting into the storm*) Blow till thou burst thy wind, if room enough!	5

Mariners *rush to work. Some exit.*

Enter Alonso, Sebastian, Antonio, Ferdinand, Gonzalo, *and others.*

Alonso	Good boatswain, have care. Where's the Master? Play the men.	10
Boatswain	I pray now, keep below.	
Antonio	Where is the Master, bosun?	
Boatswain	Do you not hear him? You mar our labour. Keep your cabins! You do assist the storm.	
Gonzalo	Nay, good, be patient.	15
Boatswain	When the sea is. Hence! What cares these roarers for the name of King? To cabin! Silence! Trouble us not!	
Gonzalo	Good, yet remember whom thou hast aboard.	
Boatswain	None that I more love than myself. You are a councillor. If you can command these elements to silence and work the peace of the present, we will not hand a rope more.	20

Two lords, Sebastian (the King's brother) and Antonio, argue with the Boatswain.

24   **if it so hap:** if that's what happens

26–8   **he hath … gallows:** i.e. everything about him suggests that he will die by hanging, not drowning

29   **rope … destiny:** hangman's rope by which he is destined to die

29–30   **doth little advantage:** i.e. our anchor is of little help to us

30–1   **our case is miserable:** our situation is desperate

33   **to try … main-course:** leave only the mainsail

34–5   **They … office:** The passengers are making more noise than the storm or the crew

36   **give o'er:** give up

38   **A pox … throat:** May a disease get your throat (Sebastian is cursing him)
     blasphemous: speaking against God

41   **cur:** dog
     whoreson: illegitimate

43   **I'll … drowning:** I guarantee he will not drown

44–5   **unstanched wench:** loose woman

46–7   **Lay her … again!:** Bring the ship's bows into the wind! Raise the foresail again!

---Think about

- What early impressions have you formed of Sebastian and Antonio from the way they speak to the ship's crew?

Use your authority! If you cannot, give thanks you have lived so long; and make yourself ready in your cabin for the mischance of the hour, if it so hap. – Cheerly, good hearts! – Out of our way, I say!   25

Exit, with MARINERS.
Exit ALONSO, *with* FERDINAND, SEBASTIAN, *and* ANTONIO *following.*

GONZALO   I have great comfort from this fellow. Methinks he hath no drowning mark upon him. His complexion is perfect gallows. Stand fast, good Fate, to his hanging. Make the rope of his destiny our cable, for our own doth little advantage. If he be not born to be hanged, our case is   30
miserable.

Exit.

Re-enter BOATSWAIN.

BOATSWAIN   Down with the topmast! Yare! Lower, lower! Bring her to try with main-course. (*A loud cry is heard*) A plague upon this howling! They are louder than the weather or our office.   35

Re-enter SEBASTIAN, ANTONIO, *and* GONZALO.

Yet again! What do you here? Shall we give o'er, and drown? Have you a mind to sink?

SEBASTIAN   A pox o' your throat, you bawling, blasphemous, incharitable dog!

BOATSWAIN   Work you, then!   40

ANTONIO   Hang, cur! Hang, you whoreson, insolent noise-maker! We are less afraid to be drowned than thou art.

GONZALO   I'll warrant him for drowning, though the ship were no stronger than a nutshell, and as leaky as an unstanched wench.   45

BOATSWAIN   Lay her a-hold, a-hold! Set her two courses! Off to sea again! Lay her off!

Storm noise increases. Enter MARINERS, *wet.*

MARINERS   All lost! To prayers, to prayers! All lost!

The force of the storm becomes so strong that the ship splits apart.

49 **What … cold?**: Are we going to die?

51 **our case … theirs**: we are in the same situation

52 **merely**: utterly
53 **wide-chapped**: big-mouthed
53–4 **would thou … tides!**: It was a common punishment to hang pirates at the water's edge and leave them there for three tides to wash over them. Antonio wants the Boatswain to take longer than that to drown.
56 **gape … him**: open its mouth as wide as it could to swallow him

62–3 **would … ground**: i.e. he would give any amount of sea for the tiniest patch of bare land
63 **long … furze**: heather and gorse
64 **fain**: gladly

Think about

• In what ways does Gonzalo seem to be different from Sebastian and Antonio? Think about his view of the Boatswain, for example.

• How would you describe Gonzalo's mood in this scene?

BOATSWAIN	What, must our mouths be cold?
GONZALO	The King and Prince at prayers! Let's assist them, 50 For our case is as theirs.
SEBASTIAN	I'm out of patience.
ANTONIO	We are merely cheated of our lives by drunkards. This wide-chapped rascal – (*To the* BOATSWAIN) would thou mightst lie drowning The washing of ten tides!
GONZALO	He'll be hanged yet, Though every drop of water swear against it, 55 And gape at wid'st to glut him.

Confusion of noise and cries: 'Mercy on us!' – 'We split, we split!' – 'Farewell, my wife and children!' – 'Farewell, brother!' – 'We split, we split, we split!'

ANTONIO	Let's all sink with the King. 60
SEBASTIAN	Let's take leave of him.

Exit SEBASTIAN, *with* ANTONIO.

GONZALO	Now would I give a thousand furlongs of sea for an acre of barren ground – long heath, broom, furze, anything! The wills above be done! But I would fain die a dry death. 65

Exeunt.

Ninagawa Company, 1992

RSC, 1998

RSC, 1998

Shakespeare's Globe, 2000

In this scene ...

- The magician Prospero tells his daughter Miranda about their past.
- He explains that he was once Duke of Milan, but that his brother Antonio had stolen the dukedom from him, helped by Alonso, King of Naples.
- Prospero reminds Ariel how he once saved the spirit from being tormented by a witch. Caliban, the witch's son, angrily curses Prospero for having stolen the island from him.
- Ariel leads in Ferdinand, King Alonso's son. He and Miranda fall in love.

On an island nearby, a young girl called Miranda is frightened for the ship's passengers, having seen the ship wrecked in the storm Prospero created. Her father Prospero, a magician, reassures her that no-one has been hurt.

1   **Art**: magic powers
2   **allay them**: quieten them
3   **pitch**: black tar-like substance
4   **But**: except
   mounting ... cheek: rising up to the face of the sky
5   **fire**: lightning
6   **brave**: fine / splendid
7   **creature**: person
11 **or ere**: before
13 **fraughting souls**: the people who made up the 'cargo' or 'freight'
   Be collected: Calm down
14 **piteous**: pitying

18–19   **nought ... I am**: knowing nothing about where I come from
19   **more better**: of higher status
20   **full poor cell**: extremely lowly dwelling

21–2   **More ... thoughts**: i.e. I never felt the need to know more than that

---

Think about

- What is your impression of Miranda from her reaction to having seen the ship wrecked? Look at lines 1 to 15.

Outside Prospero's cave on the island.

Enter PROSPERO *and* MIRANDA.

MIRANDA	If by your Art, my dearest father, you have
	Put the wild waters in this roar, allay them.
	The sky, it seems, would pour down stinking pitch,
	But that the sea, mounting to the welkin's cheek,
	Dashes the fire out. O, I have suffered

MIRANDA   If by your Art, my dearest father, you have
Put the wild waters in this roar, allay them.
The sky, it seems, would pour down stinking pitch,
But that the sea, mounting to the welkin's cheek,
Dashes the fire out. O, I have suffered   5
With those that I saw suffer! A brave vessel,
Who had, no doubt, some noble creature in her,
Dashed all to pieces! O, the cry did knock
Against my very heart! Poor souls, they perished!
Had I been any god of power, I would   10
Have sunk the sea within the earth, or ere
It should the good ship so have swallowed, and
The fraughting souls within her.

PROSPERO   Be collected.
No more amazement. Tell your piteous heart
There's no harm done.

MIRANDA   O, woe the day!

PROSPERO   No harm.   15
I have done nothing but in care of thee –
Of thee, my dear one; thee, my daughter – who
Art ignorant of what thou art; nought knowing
Of whence I am, nor that I am more better
Than Prospero, master of a full poor cell,   20
And thy no greater father.

MIRANDA   More to know
Did never meddle with my thoughts.

PROSPERO   'Tis time
I should inform thee farther. Lend thy hand,
And pluck my magic garment from me. – So.
(*He lays down his magic cloak.*)
Lie there, my Art. Wipe thou thine eyes. Have comfort.   25

Prospero says that the time is now right to tell Miranda who she is and how they came to be on the island. He tells her that, twelve years before, he was the Duke of Milan.

26   **direful spectacle**: dreadful sight

28   **provision**: careful preparation
     mine Art: my magic
29   **ordered**: arranged
29–31   **that … vessel**: that not a single person on that ship – not even a hair – has been lost
31   **Betid**: happened

35   **to … inquisition**: with questions not answered
36   **Stay**: Wait
37   **bids thee ope**: asks you to open

41   **Out**: quite

43–4   **Of any thing … remembrance**: Tell me any image you can remember

45   **an assurance**: something I am certain about
46   **That … warrants**: that my memory knows for sure
47   **tended**: looked after
50   **dark … time**: dark gulf of time that has passed
51   **aught ere**: anything from before
52   **thou may'st**: you might remember

Think about

• Prospero tells Miranda that 'The hour's now come' to tell her more about who he is and where they came from (line 36). Why is the time now right, do you think?

• What does the way Prospero and Miranda speak to one another tell us about their relationship?

	The direful spectacle of the wreck, which touched	
	The very virtue of compassion in thee,	
	I have with such provision in mine Art	
	So safely ordered that there is no soul –	
	No, not so much perdition as an hair	30
	Betid to any creature in the vessel	
	Which thou heard'st cry, which thou saw'st sink. Sit down;	
	For thou must now know farther.	

MIRANDA   You have often
Begun to tell me what I am, but stopped;
And left me to a bootless inquisition,   35
Concluding 'Stay: not yet.'

PROSPERO   The hour's now come.
The very minute bids thee ope thine ear.
Obey, and be attentive. Canst thou remember
A time before we came unto this cell?
I do not think thou canst; for then thou wast not   40
Out three years old.

MIRANDA   Certainly, sir, I can!

PROSPERO   By what? By any other house or person?
Of any thing the image tell me, that
Hath kept with thy remembrance.

MIRANDA   'Tis far off,
And rather like a dream than an assurance   45
That my remembrance warrants. Had I not
Four or five women once, that tended me?

PROSPERO   Thou hadst, and more, Miranda. But how is it
That this lives in thy mind? What see'st thou else
In the dark backward and abysm of time?   50
If thou rememb'rest aught ere thou cam'st here,
How thou cam'st here thou may'st.

MIRANDA   But that I do not.

PROSPERO   Twelve year since, Miranda, twelve year since,
Thy father was the Duke of Milan, and
A prince of power.

Prospero tells Miranda that he had handed over the government of Milan to his brother, Antonio, so that he could devote more of his time to study.

56 piece of virtue: model of chastity / sexual purity

59 no worse issued: of no less noble birth

60 from thence: away from there

63 holp hither: helped here

64 o'the teen ... you to: of the grief I have caused you

65 is ... remembrance: I cannot remember **farther**: go on

68 perfidious: treacherous
69 to him put: placed in his hands

71 Through ... first: Milan was the most important of the Italian states
73–4 for ... parallel: there was no-one to match him as a student of the arts and sciences
75 cast upon: handed over to
76–7 transported ... in: totally absorbed in
78 attend: listen to

heedfully: carefully

79 perfected: skilled in
suits: favours
80–1 t'advance ... over-topping: who to promote, who to hold back
81–3 new ... them: i.e. he promoted Prospero's followers or brought in new people
83–4 having ... office: i.e. having control over who was given which important posts
87 sucked ... on't: sucked the life out of it

Think about

• Here we are told how Prospero and Miranda came to be on the island. Who is Antonio and what part did he play in Prospero's past?

• What are Prospero's feelings about Antonio? What does the ivy image (lines 85 to 87) suggest, for example?

• How far are Prospero's feelings towards Antonio justified?

| MIRANDA | Sir, are not you my father? | 55 |

PROSPERO Thy mother was a piece of virtue, and
She said thou wast my daughter; and thy father
Was Duke of Milan – and his only heir
And princess, no worse issued.

MIRANDA O, the heavens!
What foul play had we, that we came from thence? 60
Or blessèd was't we did?

PROSPERO Both, both, my girl.
By foul play, as thou say'st, were we heaved thence –
But blessedly holp hither.

MIRANDA O, my heart bleeds
To think o'the teen that I have turned you to,
Which is from my remembrance! Please you, farther. 65

PROSPERO My brother, and thy uncle, called Antonio –
I pray thee, mark me, that a brother should
Be so perfidious! – he whom next thyself
Of all the world I loved, and to him put
The manage of my state: as at that time 70
Through all the signories it was the first,
And Prospero the prime duke, being so reputed
In dignity, and for the liberal arts
Without a parallel. Those being all my study,
The government I cast upon my brother, 75
And to my state grew stranger, being transported
And rapt in secret studies. Thy false uncle –
Dost thou attend me?

MIRANDA Sir, most heedfully.

PROSPERO – Being once perfected how to grant suits,
How to deny them, who t'advance, and who 80
To trash for over-topping, new created
The creatures that were mine, I say, or changed them,
Or else new formed them; having both the key
Of officer and office, set all hearts i'the state
To what tune pleased his ear – that now he was 85
The ivy which had hid my princely trunk,
And sucked my verdure out on't. Thou attend'st not?

While Prospero shut himself away studying in his library, Antonio's ambitions grew. He wanted to become Duke of Milan in his brother's place.

89 worldly ends: practical day-to-day matters

90 closeness: shutting myself away

91 retired: performed in secret

92 O'er-prized ... rate: was even more valuable than people estimated

94 beget: give rise to

95–6 A falsehood ... was: disloyalty in contrast to my trust in him, but equal to it in strength

97 sans bound: without limit
lorded: made into a lord

98 revenue: income

99 what ... exact: what other riches he could gain using my power

100–2 having into ... lie: Antonio was like a man who repeats a lie so often that he comes to believe it

103–5 Out ... prerogative: Because of his acting in my place and using all a ruler's powers

107–9 To have ... Milan: To destroy the barrier between acting the part of Duke and actually being Duke he decided he must really take over absolute power in Milan

110–11 Of temporal ... incapable: He thinks me unfit to exercise royal power

111 confederates: makes an alliance

112 So dry ... sway: he was so thirsty for power

113 To give ... homage: to pay the King of Naples a yearly sum of money and show that he accepted his power

114–16 Subject ... stooping: place the formerly free dukedom shamefully under the King's control

117 th'event: what then happened

Think about

- Do you think Prospero believes that he was responsible for Antonio's actions?

- How would you describe the tone of Prospero's story-telling here? Has he patiently accepted what happened to him, for example, or does he seem angry about it?

MIRANDA   O, good sir, I do.

PROSPERO   I pray thee, mark me.
            I, thus neglecting worldly ends, all dedicated
            To closeness and the bettering of my mind   **90**
            With that which, but by being so retired,
            O'er-prized all popular rate, in my false brother
            Awaked an evil nature – and my trust,
            Like a good parent, did beget of him
            A falsehood in its contrary as great   **95**
            As my trust was; which had indeed no limit,
            A confidence sans bound. He being thus lorded,
            Not only with what my revenue yielded,
            But what my power might else exact – like one
            Who having into truth, by telling of it,   **100**
            Made such a sinner of his memory,
            To credit his own lie – he did believe
            He was indeed the duke. Out o'the substitution,
            And executing th'outward face of royalty,
            With all prerogative – hence his ambition growing – **105**
            Dost thou hear?

MIRANDA   Your tale, sir, would cure deafness.

PROSPERO   – To have no screen between this part he played
            And him he played it for, he needs will be
            Absolute Milan. Me, poor man, my library
            Was dukedom large enough. Of temporal royalties   **110**
            He thinks me now incapable; confederates –
            So dry he was for sway – wi'the King of Naples
            To give him annual tribute, do him homage,
            Subject his coronet to his crown, and bend
            The dukedom, yet unbowed – alas, poor Milan! –   **115**
            To most ignoble stooping.

MIRANDA   O, the heavens!

PROSPERO   Mark his condition, and th'event: then tell me
            If this might be a brother.

MIRANDA   I should sin
            To think but nobly of my grandmother:
            Good wombs have borne bad sons.

With the support of Alonso, the King of Naples, Antonio stole Prospero's title from him and became Duke of Milan. Prospero and Miranda were cast out to sea in a fragile boat.

120 **condition**: i.e. the secret agreement Antonio made with Alonso

122 **inveterate**: deep-rooted
hearkens … suit: looks favourably on my brother's request

123–4 **in lieu … tribute**: in return for granting the King's supremacy and paying him the money

125–6 **presently … Out**: immediately drive me and my child out

128 **levied**: got together

129 **Fated … purpose**: destined to be suitable

131 **ministers … purpose**: agents employed to do the deed

134 **hint**: occasion

135 **That … to't**: which forces out tears

138 **impertinent**: irrelevant

139 **Well … wench**: Good question, my girl

140 **provokes**: makes you ask
durst: dared

144 **In few**: In short
bark: boat

146 **carcass of a butt**: remains of a tub

148 **hoist us**: 1 lifted us up into the boat; or 2 pushed us out

151 **Did … wrong**: i.e. the winds did them wrong in blowing them out to sea, but also had sympathy

— **Think about** —

• What does the image on line 143 suggest about Antonio's and Alonso's behaviour at the time?

• What do Miranda's reactions tell us about her? Look at lines 132 to 135, 138 to 139, and 151 to 152.

PROSPERO	Now the condition: 120

This King of Naples, being an enemy
To me inveterate, hearkens my brother's suit –
Which was, that he, in lieu o'the premises
Of homage and I know not how much tribute,
Should presently extirpate me and mine   125
Out of the dukedom, and confer fair Milan,
With all the honours, on my brother. Whereon,
A treacherous army levied, one midnight
Fated to the purpose, did Antonio open
The gates of Milan. And, i'the dead of darkness,   130
The ministers for the purpose hurried thence
Me and thy crying self.

MIRANDA   Alack, for pity!
I, not remembering how I cried out then,
Will cry it o'er again. It is a hint
That wrings mine eyes to't.

PROSPERO   Hear a little further,   135
And then I'll bring thee to the present business
Which now's upon us – without the which this story
Were most impertinent.

MIRANDA   Wherefore did they not
That hour destroy us?

PROSPERO   Well demanded, wench.
My tale provokes that question. Dear, they durst not,   140
So dear the love my people bore me – nor set
A mark so bloody on the business: but
With colours fairer painted their foul ends.
In few, they hurried us aboard a bark,
Bore us some leagues to sea – where they prepared   145
A rotten carcass of a butt, not rigged,
Nor tackle, sail, nor mast: the very rats
Instinctively have quit it. There they hoist us,
To cry to the sea that roared to us; to sigh
To the winds, whose pity, sighing back again,   150
Did us but loving wrong.

MIRANDA   Alack, what trouble
Was I then to you!

Prospero and Miranda were able to survive because Gonzalo kindly gave them food and water, as well as some important books from Prospero's library. Prospero's storm has now brought his enemies to the island.

152	**cherubin**: guardian angel
154	**Infusèd ... heaven**: filled with a strength which came from heaven
156–7	**raised ... stomach**: gave me the courage to keep going
158	**ensue**: follow / happen
159	**By Providence divine**: i.e. with God's help
163	**Master ... design**: the man in charge of the plan
164	**stuffs**: household goods
165	**steaded much**: been of great use **of**: out of
168–9	**Would ... man**: I wish I could see that man one day
172	**made ... profit**: i.e. given you a better education
177	**thus far forth**: this much
180	**prescience**: i.e. ability to see into the future
181–2	**my zenith ... star**: the stars look right for me to achieve my greatest success
182–4	**whose ... droop**: if I do not take advantage of this opportunity, I will never again be successful

Think about

- In Prospero's story, in what ways does Gonzalo seem to be different from Antonio and Alonso?

- What dramatic purpose do Miranda's questions serve?

42

PROSPERO	O, a cherubin
	Thou wast that did preserve me! Thou didst smile,
	Infusèd with a fortitude from heaven,
	When I have decked the sea with drops full salt, 155
	Under my burden groaned – which raised in me
	An undergoing stomach, to bear up
	Against what should ensue.
MIRANDA	How came we ashore?
PROSPERO	By Providence divine.
	Some food we had, and some fresh water, that 160
	A noble Neapolitan, Gonzalo,
	Out of his charity, who being then appointed
	Master of this design, did give us – with
	Rich garments, linens, stuffs and necessaries,
	Which since have steaded much. So, of his gentleness, 165
	Knowing I loved my books, he furnished me
	From mine own library with volumes that
	I prize above my dukedom.
MIRANDA	Would I might
	But ever see that man!
PROSPERO	Now I arise.
	Sit still, and hear the last of our sea-sorrow. 170
	(He stands, and puts on his magic cloak again.)
	Here in this island we arrived – and here
	Have I, thy schoolmaster, made thee more profit
	Than other princesses can, that have more time
	For vainer hours, and tutors not so careful.
MIRANDA	Heavens thank you for't! And now, I pray you, sir. 175
	For still 'tis beating in my mind, your reason
	For raising this sea-storm?
PROSPERO	Know thus far forth.
	By accident most strange, bountiful Fortune
	Now my dear lady, hath mine enemies
	Brought to this shore. And by my prescience 180
	I find my zenith doth depend upon
	A most auspicious star, whose influence
	If now I court not, but omit, my fortunes
	Will ever after droop. Here cease more questions:

Prospero makes Miranda sleep and calls for Ariel, a spirit who is his servant. Prospero hears that it was Ariel who created the storm, as he had ordered. Ariel then appeared on the ship like a flame, driving all the passengers overboard in terror.

185 **good dullness**: a drowsiness that is good for you

186 **give it way**: give in to it

187 **Come away**: Come here

192–3 **task Ariel**: give Ariel work to do

193 **quality**: companion spirits

194 **to point**: exactly
bade: commanded

195 **To every article**: In every detail

198 **flamed amazement**: appeared to them as terrifying fire

200 **yards**: poles on which the sails are set
bowsprit: spar extending forward from the bows of a boat

201 **Jove's**: Jupiter's

201–2 **precursors O'**: things that come before

202–3 **more ... not**: i.e. Ariel's flames were as fast as lightning and as difficult to catch sight of

203–6 **The fire ... shake**: i.e. the cracks of thunder, with its smell of sulphur, seemed to surround Neptune (Roman god of the sea, who carried a three-pronged spear)

207 **constant**: determined
coil: confused noise

209–10 **played ... desperation**: did things typical of desperate people

211 **brine**: salty sea

213 **up-staring**: standing on end

Think about

- At this point there is no explanation of who or what Ariel, Prospero's 'servant', is. What does Ariel seem to be able to do? What kind of being does Ariel seem to be?

- How do Ariel's speeches here convey a sense of pace and movement? For example, look at the verbs in lines 190 to 192 and 208 to 215, and the 'place' phrases in lines 196 to 201.

Thou art inclined to sleep. 'Tis a good dullness,   185
And give it way. I know thou canst not choose.

MIRANDA *falls asleep.*

Come away, servant, come. I am ready now.
Approach, my Ariel, come.

Enter ARIEL.

ARIEL   All hail, great master! Grave sir, hail! I come
             To answer thy best pleasure – be't to fly,   190
             To swim, to dive into the fire, to ride
             On the curled clouds. To thy strong bidding task
             Ariel and all his quality.

PROSPERO   Hast thou, spirit,
             Performed to point the tempest that I bade thee?

ARIEL   To every article.   195
             I boarded the King's ship. Now on the beak,
             Now in the waist, the deck, in every cabin,
             I flamed amazement. Sometime I'd divide,
             And burn in many places. On the topmast,
             The yards and bowsprit would I flame distinctly,   200
             Then meet and join. Jove's lightnings, the precursors
             O'the dreadful thunder-claps, more momentary
             And sight-outrunning were not. The fire and cracks
             Of sulphurous roaring the most mighty Neptune
             Seemed to besiege, and make his bold waves tremble – 205
             Yea, his dread trident shake.

PROSPERO   My brave spirit!
             Who was so firm, so constant, that this coil
             Would not infect his reason?

ARIEL   Not a soul
             But felt a fever of the mad, and played
             Some tricks of desperation. All but mariners   210
             Plunged in the foaming brine, and quit the vessel,
             Then all afire with me. The King's son, Ferdinand,
             With hair up-staring – then like reeds, not hair –
             Was the first man that leaped; cried, 'Hell is empty,
             And all the devils are here!'

Ariel confirms that no-one has been harmed. A spell on the crew has left them asleep on the ship. The survivors are all on the island in groups, except for Ferdinand, the King's son, who is alone.

216 nigh: near

218 sustaining garments: clothes that kept them afloat
220 troops: groups

223 odd angle: out-of-the-way corner
224 in this sad knot: i.e. Ariel folds his arms as a sign of sadness
224–5 Of the … disposed: Tell me what you have done with the sailors and the King's ship

227 nook: inlet

229 still-vexed: always stormy
230 under hatches: below deck
231 with … labour: with the effect of a magic spell added to their exhaustion

234 flote: sea

Think about

• Although Prospero himself has magic power, it is Ariel who enacts his commands. What part has the spirit played in the crucial act of bringing Alonso, Antonio, and the others on shore?

• Why might Prospero have instructed Ariel to disperse the ship's passengers in separate groups around the island?

237 thy charge: what you have been asked to do

239 mid season: noon
240 two glasses: two hours, i.e. at least two hours past noon
241 preciously: carefully, i.e. we must not waste a moment
242 pains: difficult work
243 remember: remind

PROSPERO	Why, that's my spirit! 215
	But was not this nigh shore?
ARIEL	Close by, my master.
PROSPERO	But are they, Ariel, safe?
ARIEL	Not a hair perished:
	On their sustaining garments not a blemish,
	But fresher than before. And, as thou bad'st me,
	In troops I have dispersed them 'bout the isle. 220
	The King's son have I landed by himself –
	Whom I left cooling of the air with sighs
	In an odd angle of the isle, and sitting,
	His arms in this sad knot. (***He folds his arms.***)
PROSPERO	Of the King's ship,
	The mariners, say how thou hast disposed, 225
	And all the rest o'the fleet.
ARIEL	Safely in the harbour
	Is the King's ship. In the deep nook, where once
	Thou call'dst me up at midnight to fetch dew
	From the still-vexed Bermudas, there she's hid.
	The mariners all under hatches stowed – 230
	Who, with a charm joined to their suffered labour,
	I have left asleep. And for the rest o'the fleet,
	Which I dispersed, they all have met again,
	And are upon the Mediterranean flote,
	Bound sadly home for Naples – 235
	Supposing that they saw the King's ship wrecked,
	And his great person perish.
PROSPERO	Ariel, thy charge
	Exactly is performed. But there's more work.
	What is the time o'the day?
ARIEL	Past the mid season.
PROSPERO	At least two glasses. The time 'twixt six and now 240
	Must by us both be spent most preciously.
ARIEL	Is there more toil? Since thou dost give me pains,
	Let me remember thee what thou hast promised,
	Which is not yet performed me.

Ariel asks Prospero not to forget his promise to release the spirit from being Prospero's servant. Prospero angrily reminds Ariel how he freed the spirit from a spell cast by the witch Sycorax.

246 Before ... out?: Before the time is up?

250 bate me: reduce the time I would have to serve you by

252 think'st ... to: you resent having to
252–3 ooze ... deep: muddy bed of the sea

255 veins: underground streams / channels
256 baked: hard

257 malignant: wicked

259 a hoop: i.e. her body was bent double

264 mischiefs manifold: many different wicked acts
266–7 For ... life: Her life was spared because of one good thing she had done

---Think about---

• What gives Prospero his power over Ariel? What does Ariel owe him?

• From what you have seen so far, how would you describe the relationship between Prospero and Ariel? For example, think about what sort of master Prospero seems to be.

• Look at the line divisions on this page. How do they help to create tension in the dialogue?

PROSPERO	How now, moody? What is't thou canst demand?
ARIEL	My liberty. 245
PROSPERO	Before the time be out? No more!
ARIEL	I prithee, Remember I have done thee worthy service; Told thee no lies, made no mistakings, served Without or grudge or grumblings. Thou did promise To bate me a full year.
PROSPERO	Dost thou forget 250 From what a torment I did free thee?
ARIEL	No!
PROSPERO	Thou dost – and think'st it much to tread the ooze Of the salt deep, To run upon the sharp wind of the north, To do me business in the veins o' the earth 255 When it is baked with frost.
ARIEL	I do not, sir.
PROSPERO	Thou liest, malignant thing! Hast thou forgot The foul witch Sycorax, who with age and envy Was grown into a hoop? Hast thou forgot her?
ARIEL	No, sir.
PROSPERO	Thou hast. Where was she born? Speak. Tell me! 260
ARIEL	Sir, in Algiers.
PROSPERO	O, was she so? I must Once in a month recount what thou hast been, Which thou forget'st. This damned witch Sycorax, For mischiefs manifold, and sorceries terrible To enter human hearing, from Algiers, 265 Thou know'st, was banished. For one thing she did They would not take her life. Is not this true?
ARIEL	Ay, sir.

Ariel had been trapped inside a pine tree by the witch, Sycorax, who then died. When Prospero used his magic to release Ariel, Sycorax's son, Caliban, was the only other creature living on the island. Prospero promises to release Ariel in two days' time.

269 **blue-eyed**: blue eyelids were a sign of pregnancy

272 **for**: because
273 **abhorred**: disgusting
274 **grand hests**: great commands
275 **potent ministers**: powerful spirits
276 **unmitigable**: that could not be soothed
277 **cloven**: split open
     rift: split
280 **vent**: utter / emit
281 **as mill-wheels strike**: as mill-wheel blades hit the water
282 **Save**: except
283 **whelp hag-born**: young dog, born of a witch

291 **mine Art**: my magic
292 **made gape**: opened up

294 **murmur'st**: complain
     rend: open up
295 **entrails**: insides

297 **be ... command**: do exactly as you ask
298 **gently**: politely

299 **discharge**: free

Think about

- Why do you think Ariel seems so keen to be free from serving Prospero?

- We learn about a new character, Caliban. What is his background?

50

PROSPERO	This blue-eyed hag was hither brought with child,	
	And here was left by the sailors. Thou, my slave,	270
	As thou report'st thyself, wast then her servant.	
	And, for thou wast a spirit too delicate	
	To act her earthy and abhorred commands,	
	Refusing her grand hests, she did confine thee,	
	By help of her more potent ministers,	275
	And in her most unmitigable rage,	
	Into a cloven pine. Within which rift	
	Imprisoned thou didst painfully remain	
	A dozen years; within which space she died,	
	And left thee there – where thou didst vent thy groans	280
	As fast as mill-wheels strike. Then was this island –	
	Save for the son that she did litter here,	
	A freckled whelp hag-born – not honoured with	
	A human shape.	

ARIEL   Yes, Caliban her son.

PROSPERO	Dull thing, I say so: he, that Caliban,	285
	Whom now I keep in service. Thou best know'st	
	What torment I did find thee in. Thy groans	
	Did make wolves howl, and penetrate the breasts	
	Of ever-angry bears. It was a torment	
	To lay upon the damned, which Sycorax	290
	Could not again undo. It was mine Art,	
	When I arrived and heard thee, that made gape	
	The pine, and let thee out.	

ARIEL   I thank thee, master.

PROSPERO	If thou more murmur'st, I will rend an oak,	
	And peg thee in his knotty entrails, till	295
	Thou hast howled away twelve winters.	

ARIEL   Pardon, master.
                     I will be correspondent to command,
                     And do my spiriting gently.

PROSPERO   Do so!
                     And after two days I will discharge thee.

ARIEL	That's my noble master! What shall I do?	300
	Say what! What shall I do?	

Prospero orders Ariel to change shape and become invisible. Prospero wakes Miranda up and then calls Caliban.

301–2 **make ... Like**: take on the appearance of

302 **nymph**: female sea-spirit

302–4 **Be subject ... else**: i.e. Ariel will be visible only to himself and to Prospero

308 **Heaviness**: sleepiness

310 **Yields**: gives

312 **miss**: do without

313–4 **serves ... us**: does jobs which are useful to us

317 **tortoise**: i.e. Caliban is being slow

318 **quaint**: skilful

320 **got**: fathered

321 **dam**: mother

Think about

Caliban's appearance is never clearly described and stage and film productions have represented him in a wide variety of ways.

• Look at the photographs on pages 12 to 13. What differences are there between these versions of Caliban?

• How would you choose to present him, from what you know so far?

PROSPERO	Go make thyself
	Like a nymph o' the sea. Be subject to
	No sight but thine and mine: invisible
	To every eyeball else. Go take this shape,
	And hither come in't. Go! Hence, with diligence! 305

Exit ARIEL.

(*To* MIRANDA) Awake, dear heart, awake! Thou hast
  slept well.
Awake!

MIRANDA	The strangeness of your story put
	Heaviness in me.
PROSPERO	Shake it off. Come on:
	We'll visit Caliban my slave, who never
	Yields us kind answer.
MIRANDA	'Tis a villain, sir, 310
	I do not love to look on.
PROSPERO	But as 'tis,
	We cannot miss him. He does make our fire,
	Fetch in our wood, and serves in offices
	That profit us. What, ho! Slave! Caliban!
	Thou earth, thou: speak!
CALIBAN	(*Calling from the far side of Prospero's cave*)
	There's wood enough within! 315
PROSPERO	Come forth, I say! There's other business for thee.
	Come, thou tortoise! When?

Enter ARIEL, *like a water-nymph.*

Fine apparition! My quaint Ariel,
Hark in thine ear. (*He whispers instructions to* ARIEL.)

ARIEL	My lord, it shall be done.

Exit.

PROSPERO	Thou poisonous slave, got by the devil himself 320
	Upon thy wicked dam, come forth!

Caliban curses Prospero who threatens to torment him as punishment. Caliban complains that Prospero has stolen the island from him. Prospero replies that he had treated Caliban well until he tried to rape Miranda.

Think about

- Caliban says 'This island's mine ...' (lines 332 to 333). Is it? Has Prospero done wrong by taking control of the island and treating Caliban as a slave, in your opinion? In what ways did Caliban help Prospero when he first arrived on the island?

- How would you describe Caliban's language? What does it tell us about him? Think about (a) his use of vocabulary to do with the natural world; and (b) his use of simple, single-syllable words.

323 **raven**: a bird associated with witchcraft and evil
unwholesome fen: unhealthy bog
324 **south-west**: wind thought to bring diseases

327 **pen thy breath up**: make it impossible for you to breathe
urchins: spirits in the shape of hedgehogs
328 **vast**: long stretch
329 **All ... thee**: i.e. will torment you

336 **bigger ... less**: i.e. the sun and the moon
338 **qualities**: features / characteristics
339 **brine-pits**: i.e. how to avoid salty water
340 **charms**: spells
341 **light**: come down

343 **sty me**: keep me shut up like a pig

346 **stripes**: whipping
used: treated
348–9 **to violate ... child**: to rape Miranda

350 **Would't ... done**: I wish I had done it
351 **I ... else**: i.e. otherwise Caliban's children would have become the island's population
352 **Abhorrèd**: Disgusting
353 **print**: i.e. influence

Enter CALIBAN.

CALIBAN	As wicked dew as e'er my mother brushed
	With raven's feather from unwholesome fen
	Drop on you both! A south-west blow on ye
	And blister you all o'er! 325

PROSPERO	For this, be sure, tonight thou shalt have cramps,
	Side-stitches that shall pen thy breath up: urchins
	Shall, for that vast of night that they may work,
	All exercise on thee. Thou shalt be pinched
	As thick as honeycomb, each pinch more stinging 330
	Than bees that made 'em.

CALIBAN	I must eat my dinner.
	This island's mine, by Sycorax my mother,
	Which thou tak'st from me. When thou cam'st first,
	Thou strok'st me, and made much of me; wouldst give me
	Water with berries in't; and teach me how 335
	To name the bigger light, and how the less,
	That burn by day and night. And then I loved thee,
	And showed thee all the qualities o'the isle,
	The fresh springs, brine-pits, barren place and fertile.
	Cursed be I that did so! All the charms 340
	Of Sycorax, toads, beetles, bats, light on you!
	For I am all the subjects that you have,
	Which first was mine own king! And here you sty me
	In this hard rock, whiles you do keep from me
	The rest o'the island.

PROSPERO	Thou most lying slave, 345
	Whom stripes may move, not kindness! I have used thee,
	Filth as thou art, with human care; and lodged thee
	In mine own cell, till thou didst seek to violate
	The honour of my child.

CALIBAN	O ho! O ho! Would't had been done! 350
	Thou didst prevent me. I had peopled else
	This isle with Calibans!

MIRANDA	Abhorrèd slave,
	Which any print of goodness wilt not take,
	Being capable of all ill! I pitied thee,

Miranda reminds Caliban that she taught him how to speak. When Prospero orders him to fetch in fuel, Caliban unwillingly obeys because he is afraid of Prospero's power.

358–9 **endowed … known**: I gave you the language to express yourself
359 **race**: nature (inherited character)

361 **abide**: bear

363 **more than a prison**: a more extreme punishment
364 **my profit on't**: the benefit I have got from it
365 **red plague**: red sores from the plague
      rid: destroy
366 **Hag-seed**: child of a witch
367 **thou'rt best**: if you know what's good for you
368 **answer … business**: perform the other tasks that you are told to do
      Shrug'st … malice?: Are you shrugging at me, you evil creature?
370 **rack**: torment
      old: such as old people suffer

374 **Setebos**: his mother Sycorax's god
375 **vassal**: humble servant

—**Think about**—

• What do Miranda's words to Caliban (lines 352 to 363) reveal about her feelings? Some people have thought that this speech should be spoken by Prospero. Does it seem too harsh for Miranda, in your opinion?

• What does the use of language about pain and torment tell you about Caliban's existence and his attitude to others? Look at lines 322 to 331, 340 to 341, 345 to 350, 361 to 365 and 369 to 372.

379 **whist**: grow silent
380 **Foot it featly**: Dance nimbly
381–2 **sprites … burthen**: spirits will sing the refrain

Took pains to make thee speak, taught thee each hour   355
One thing or other. When thou didst not, savage,
Know thine own meaning, but wouldst gabble like
A thing most brutish, I endowed thy purposes
With words that made them known. But thy vile race,
Though thou didst learn, had that in't which good
    natures   360
Could not abide to be with. Therefore wast thou
Deservedly confined into this rock,
Who hadst deserved more than a prison.

CALIBAN   You taught me language – and my profit on't
Is, I know how to curse. The red plague rid you   365
For learning me your language!

PROSPERO   Hag-seed, hence!
Fetch us in fuel – and be quick, thou'rt best,
To answer other business. Shrug'st thou, malice?
If thou neglect'st, or dost unwillingly
What I command, I'll rack thee with old cramps,   370
Fill all thy bones with aches, make thee roar,
That beasts shall tremble at thy din.

CALIBAN   No, pray thee.
(*Aside*) I must obey. His Art is of such power,
It would control my dam's god, Setebos,
And make a vassal of him.

PROSPERO   So, slave: hence!   375

                            Exit CALIBAN.

Re-enter ARIEL (*invisible to all except* PROSPERO), *playing and singing. He leads* FERDINAND.

ARIEL (*Song*)

Come unto these yellow sands
    And then take hands:
Curtsied when you have, and kissed,
    The wild waves whist.
Foot it featly here and there,   380
    And sweet sprites bear
The burthen. Hark, hark!
    (*Other spirit voices in the air*) Bow-wow!

The invisible Ariel leads in Ferdinand, who is enchanted by the spirit's singing. The song tells Ferdinand that his father, King Alonso, has drowned. When Miranda first sees Ferdinand, she thinks *he* is a spirit.

Think about

- What kind of mood would you want to create with Ariel's song? What sort of music would suit it?

- As you read the play, note the various ways in which all the characters from the King's ship seem to 'suffer a sea-change' (line 403).

387 **strain ... chanticleer**: tune of the boastful cock

391 **waits upon**: i.e. is played for

393 **Weeping ... wreck**: weeping over and over the death of my father in the shipwreck
395 **Allaying**: calming
396 **air**: tune

399 **Full fathom five**: At least nine metres deep

402 **fade**: decay

405 **knell**: death-bell

409 **does remember**: calls to mind
410 **no mortal business**: i.e. it must be supernatural
411 **owes**: owns
412 **The fringèd ... advance**: Open your eyes
413 **yond**: over there

415 **brave**: handsome
416 **wench**: my girl
417 **gallant**: fine gentleman
418 **but he's something**: except that he's rather

The watch-dogs bark:
(*Other spirit voices*) Bow-wow!   385
Hark, hark! I hear
     The strain of strutting chanticleer
Cry cock-a-diddle-dow:
     (*Other spirit voices*) Cock-a-diddle-dow!

FERDINAND   Where should this music be? I'the air or the earth?   390
It sounds no more; and, sure, it waits upon
Some god o'the island. Sitting on a bank,
Weeping again the King my father's wreck,
This music crept by me upon the waters,
Allaying both their fury and my passion   395
With its sweet air. Thence I have followed it –
Or it hath drawn me rather. But 'tis gone.
No, it begins again.

ARIEL *(Song)*

Full fathom five thy father lies –
     Of his bones are coral made;   400
Those are pearls that were his eyes.
     Nothing of him that doth fade,
But doth suffer a sea-change
Into something rich and strange.
Sea-nymphs hourly ring his knell –   405
     (*Chorus of spirit voices*) Ding dong –
Hark! Now I hear them –
     (ARIEL *and spirit voices*) Ding dong bell.

FERDINAND   The ditty does remember my drowned father.
This is no mortal business, nor no sound   410
That the earth owes. I hear it now above me.

PROSPERO   (*To* MIRANDA) The fringèd curtains of thine eye advance,
And say what thou see'st yond.

MIRANDA   What is't? A spirit?
Lord, how it looks about! Believe me, sir,
It carries a brave form. But 'tis a spirit.   415

PROSPERO   No, wench: it eats and sleeps and hath such senses
As we have, such. This gallant which thou see'st
Was in the wreck – and, but he's something stained

59

Miranda is immediately captivated by the sight of Ferdinand, and he is equally impressed by her. He tells her that, as his father has drowned, he is now King of Naples.

419 beauty's canker: a thing that spoils beauty

420 goodly: good-looking

422–3 for … noble: for I never saw anything in the natural world so noble-looking

423–4 It goes … it: It's happening just as I would wish

426 On whom … attend: who is served by these tunes
Vouchsafe: Please grant that

429 bear me: behave appropriately
prime: most important

431 maid or no: i.e. a human or a goddess (or possibly: unmarried or not)

433 the best: the highest-ranking person

435 What wert thou: What do you think would happen to you

436 A single thing: 1 a solitary person; 2 one and the same thing as the King of Naples

438 Myself am Naples: I am King of Naples

439 ne'er … ebb: i.e. his eyes have not been dry

442 twain: two of them

443 control: contradict

Think about

- Do Miranda and Ferdinand seem to be falling in love of their own free will, or is everything they do being controlled by Prospero?

- If you were directing this scene, where would you place Prospero on stage? What effect would you try to achieve?

	With grief (that's beauty's canker), thou might'st call him
	A goodly person. He hath lost his fellows,
	And strays about to find 'em.

With grief (that's beauty's canker), thou might'st call him
A goodly person. He hath lost his fellows,   420
And strays about to find 'em.

MIRANDA   I might call him
A thing divine, for nothing natural
I ever saw so noble.

PROSPERO   (*Aside*) It goes on, I see,
As my soul prompts it. (*To* ARIEL) Spirit, fine spirit! I'll
    free thee
Within two days for this.

FERDINAND   (*Seeing* MIRANDA) Most sure the goddess   425
On whom these airs attend! Vouchsafe my prayer
May know if you remain upon this island –
And that you will some good instruction give
How I may bear me here. My prime request,
Which I do last pronounce, is – O, you wonder! –   430
If you be maid or no?

MIRANDA   No wonder, sir;
But certainly a maid.

FERDINAND   My language! Heavens!
I am the best of them that speak this speech,
Were I but where 'tis spoken.

PROSPERO   How, the best?
What wert thou, if the King of Naples heard thee?   435

FERDINAND   A single thing, as I am now, that wonders
To hear thee speak of Naples. He does hear me –
And that he does I weep. Myself am Naples,
Who with mine eyes, ne'er since at ebb, beheld
The King my father wrecked.

MIRANDA   Alack, for mercy!   440

FERDINAND   Yes, faith, and all his lords – the Duke of Milan
And his brave son being twain.

PROSPERO   (*Aside*) The Duke of Milan
And his more braver daughter could control thee,
If now 'twere fit to do't. At the first sight

Miranda and Ferdinand have fallen in love, but Prospero wants to create obstacles so that Ferdinand does not win Miranda too easily. He therefore accuses Ferdinand of being a traitor and puts a spell on him to make him powerless.

445 **changed eyes**: i.e. fallen in love

447 **done … wrong**: 1 behaved badly; 2 made a mistake

450 **sighed for**: i.e. sighed from love

452 **affection … forth**: you have not given your love to anyone else

453 **Soft**: Wait / Be quiet a moment
454 **either's**: each other's

455 **uneasy**: more difficult
       light: easy
456 **light**: devalued
       charge: command
457 **attend**: listen to
       usurp: wrongly claim
458 **ow'st**: own

461 **temple**: i.e. Ferdinand's body
462 **ill spirit**: devil

Think about

• Why is Prospero reluctant to allow the love between Miranda and Ferdinand to develop smoothly and quickly? Look at lines 454 to 456.

• How could you show in a performance that Ferdinand is prevented from moving by Prospero's magic (line 470)?

465 **manacle**: chain

469 **entertainment**: treatment

	They have changed eyes. Delicate Ariel,	445
	I'll set thee free for this. (*To* FERDINAND) A word, good sir.	
	I fear you have done yourself some wrong. A word.	

MIRANDA (*Aside*) Why speaks my father so ungently? This
Is the third man that e'er I saw – the first
That e'er I sighed for. Pity move my father   450
To be inclined my way!

FERDINAND   O, if a virgin,
And your affection not gone forth, I'll make you
The Queen of Naples!

PROSPERO   Soft, sir! One word more.
(*Aside*) They are both in either's powers. But this swift
   business
I must uneasy make, lest too light winning   455
Make the prize light. (*To* FERDINAND) One word more:
   I charge thee
That thou attend me. Thou dost here usurp
The name thou ow'st not – and hast put thyself
Upon this island as a spy, to win it
From me, the lord on't.

FERDINAND   No, as I am a man!   460

MIRANDA There's nothing ill can dwell in such a temple.
If the ill spirit have so fair a house,
Good things will strive to dwell with't.

PROSPERO   (*To* FERDINAND) Follow me!
(*To* MIRANDA) Speak not you for him; he's a traitor. (*To*
   FERDINAND) Come!
I'll manacle thy neck and feet together.   465
Sea-water shalt thou drink: thy food shall be
The fresh-brook mussels, withered roots, and husks
Wherein the acorn cradled. Follow!

FERDINAND   No!
I will resist such entertainment till
Mine enemy has more power.

He draws his sword but is prevented from moving by
PROSPERO'*s magic power.*

Prospero continues to speak angrily with Ferdinand, who is still under his spell. Ferdinand is prepared to accept his treatment by Prospero, as well as his father's death, so long as he can see Miranda once a day.

471 **rash**: hasty
472 **gentle**: 1 not violent; 2 of noble birth
   not fearful: 1 not frightening; 2 not a coward
473 **My ... tutor?**: i.e. is a daughter telling her father what to do?
   up: away
475 **Come ... ward**: Lower your sword

477 **Beseech**: I beg

479 **I'll ... surety**: I'll guarantee his good behaviour
480 **chide thee**: speak sharply to you
481 **An advocate**: i.e. are you arguing for him

484 **To ... men**: Compared with most men

485 **affections**: i.e. feelings for Ferdinand

487 **goodlier**: better looking

488 **Thy nerves ... infancy**: Your muscles are like a child's
489 **vigour**: strength

491–5 **My father's ... maid**: i.e. all his losses and torments don't matter, if he can just see Miranda once a day
495–7 **All corners ... prison**: people who want to be free can wander through the rest of the world; this prison is room enough for me

---Think about---

• What do you think about the way Prospero speaks to Miranda in lines 479 to 480? Is he unnecessarily harsh? Merely strict? Or is it all an act?

MIRANDA	O dear father!	470

Make not too rash a trial of him, for
He's gentle, and not fearful.

PROSPERO   What! I say –
My foot my tutor? (*To* FERDINAND) Put thy sword up,
    traitor –
Who mak'st a show, but dar'st not strike, thy conscience
Is so possessed with guilt. Come from thy ward –   475
For I can here disarm thee with this stick
And make thy weapon drop.

MIRANDA   Beseech you, father!

PROSPERO   Hence! Hang not on my garments.

MIRANDA   Sir, have pity!
I'll be his surety.

PROSPERO   Silence! One word more
Shall make me chide thee, if not hate thee. What!   480
An advocate for an impostor! Hush!
Thou think'st there is no more such shapes as he,
Having seen but him and Caliban. Foolish wench!
To the most of men this is a Caliban,
And they to him are angels.

MIRANDA   My affections   485
Are then most humble. I have no ambition
To see a goodlier man.

PROSPERO   (*To* FERDINAND) Come on! Obey.
Thy nerves are in their infancy again,
And have no vigour in them.

FERDINAND   So they are.
My spirits, as in a dream, are all bound up.   490
My father's loss, the weakness which I feel,
The wreck of all my friends, nor this man's threats,
To whom I am subdued, are but light to me,
Might I but through my prison once a day
Behold this maid. All corners else o'the earth   495
Let liberty make use of: space enough
Have I in such a prison.

Prospero praises Ariel and gives him further instructions. He leads Ferdinand away.

501 **unwonted**: unusual

503 **then**: i.e. if you want your freedom

504 **To the syllable**: In every detail

---Think about ────────

• What is your impression of Prospero at the end of this first Act? Think about his relationships with Miranda, Ariel, Caliban, and Ferdinand.

PROSPERO	(*Aside*) It works. (*To* FERDINAND) Come on.
	(*To* ARIEL) Thou hast done well, fine Ariel! (*To* FERDINAND)
	   Follow me.
	(*To* ARIEL, *whispering more instructions*) Hark what
	   thou else shalt do me.

MIRANDA	(*To* FERDINAND) Be of comfort. My father's of a better nature, sir, **500** Than he appears by speech. This is unwonted Which now came from him.
PROSPERO	(*To* ARIEL) Thou shalt be as free As mountain winds. But then exactly do All points of my command.
ARIEL	To the syllable.
PROSPERO	(*To* FERDINAND) Come, follow. (*To* MIRANDA) Speak not for him. **505**

Exeunt.

In this scene ...

- Alonso and his lords are now wandering around the island.
- Alonso believes that his son, Ferdinand, is dead. Sebastian torments Alonso by suggesting that he was responsible.
- When Ariel charms most of the company asleep, Antonio persuades Sebastian to murder Alonso and replace him as King of Naples.
- As Sebastian and Antonio draw their swords to kill the sleeping Alonso and Gonzalo, Ariel causes everyone to wake up.

The ship's passengers are now shipwrecked on the island. Gonzalo attempts to comfort King Alonso but is mocked by Sebastian (Alonso's brother) and Antonio (Prospero's brother).

1 **Beseech**: I beg

3 **Is much beyond**: more than makes up for
   hint of: reason for
5 **some merchant**: some merchant ship
6 **theme of**: reason for

8–9 **weigh ... comfort**: weigh up what we have lost against the fact that we have survived

12 **visitor ... so**: i.e. Gonzalo is like a visitor to the sick who will not leave the bedside

16 **One! – Tell**: i.e. Gonzalo's wit has struck one – now keep count
17–18 **When every ... entertainer**: If a person gives in to every cause of grief that comes his way
19 **A dollar**: i.e. the 'entertainer' receives a dollar in payment
20 **Dolour**: Sadness
21 **purposed**: intended

24 **spendthrift**: waster, i.e. doesn't he talk a lot
25 **spare**: stop

Think about

- Gonzalo makes a pun of the words 'dolour' (sadness) and 'dollar' (lines 19 to 20). How can word-play like that be clearly conveyed to a modern audience? Think about whether actors might use actions or gestures, for example.

Another part of the island.

Enter ALONSO, SEBASTIAN, ANTONIO, GONZALO, ADRIAN,

FRANCISCO, *and others.*

GONZALO	(*To* ALONSO) Beseech you, sir, be merry. You have
	cause –
	So have we all – of joy; for our escape
	Is much beyond our loss. Our hint of woe
	Is common: every day, some sailor's wife,
	The masters of some merchant, and the merchant, 5
	Have just our theme of woe. But for the miracle,
	I mean our preservation, few in millions
	Can speak like us. Then wisely, good sir, weigh
	Our sorrow with our comfort.
ALONSO	Prithee, peace!
SEBASTIAN	(*Aside to* ANTONIO) He receives comfort like cold 10 porridge.
ANTONIO	(*To* SEBASTIAN) The visitor will not give him o'er so.
SEBASTIAN	(*To* ANTONIO) Look, he's winding up the watch of his wit. By and by it will strike.
GONZALO	(*To* ALONSO) Sir – 15
SEBASTIAN	One! – Tell.
GONZALO	When every grief is entertained that's offered, Comes to the entertainer –
SEBASTIAN	A dollar.
GONZALO	Dolour comes to him, indeed. You have spoken truer 20 than you purposed.
SEBASTIAN	You have taken it wiselier than I meant you should.
GONZALO	(*To* ALONSO) Therefore, my lord –
ANTONIO	Fie, what a spendthrift is he of his tongue!
ALONSO	I prithee, spare. 25

Gonzalo and another lord, Adrian, admire the island's pleasant climate and plants, but Sebastian and Antonio see it as foul-smelling, dry and bare.

34   **A match!**: It's a bet!

35   **desert**: uninhabited / empty

41   **He ... it**: He was bound to say that

42–3   **of subtle ... temperance**: of a mild and pleasant climate

44   **Temperance ... wench**: Temperance was also a girl's name in Shakespeare's time.

45   **subtle**: cunning / sly

48   **fen**: unhealthy marsh

49   **advantageous to**: good for

50   **save**: except

52   **lush and lusty**: rich and vigorous

53   **tawny**: brown / dried-out

Think about

• What bet does Antonio make with Sebastian? In what way is Antonio 'paid' when he wins (line 37)?

• Why does Gonzalo experience the island as healthy and fruitful, while Antonio sees it as foul-smelling and barren?

GONZALO	Well, I have done. But yet –	
SEBASTIAN	He will be talking.	
ANTONIO	Which, of he or Adrian, for a good wager, first begins to crow?	
SEBASTIAN	The old cock.	30
ANTONIO	The cockerel.	
SEBASTIAN	Done. The wager?	
ANTONIO	A laughter.	
SEBASTIAN	A match!	
ADRIAN	Though this island seem to be desert –	35
ANTONIO	Ha, ha, ha!	
SEBASTIAN	So: you're paid.	
ADRIAN	Uninhabitable, and almost inaccessible –	
SEBASTIAN	Yet –	
ADRIAN	Yet –	40
ANTONIO	He could not miss it.	
ADRIAN	It must needs be of subtle, tender and delicate temperance.	
ANTONIO	Temperance was a delicate wench.	
SEBASTIAN	Ay, and a subtle, as he most learnedly delivered.	45
ADRIAN	The air breathes upon us here most sweetly.	
SEBASTIAN	As if it had lungs – and rotten ones.	
ANTONIO	Or as 'twere perfumed by a fen.	
GONZALO	Here is everything advantageous to life.	
ANTONIO	True – save means to live.	50
SEBASTIAN	Of that there's none, or little.	
GONZALO	How lush and lusty the grass looks! How green!	
ANTONIO	The ground, indeed, is tawny.	

Gonzalo says how surprised he is that their clothes are as fresh and unstained as when they put them on for the marriage of Alonso's daughter to the King of Tunis in north Africa. Sebastian and Antonio, however, continue to mock his ideas.

54 **eye**: tinge / hint

56 **No ... totally**: No, he just gets it completely wrong
57 **the rarity of it**: the strange thing about it
58 **credit**: belief
59 **vouched rarities**: strange things that people swear to be true

61 **notwithstanding**: nonetheless
    glosses: brightness

65 **pocket up**: hide

68 **Tunis**: a city in north Africa

71 **paragon**: model of excellence

73 **Dido**: a Queen of Carthage who killed herself when the Trojan prince Aeneas deserted her

78 **study of**: think about

Think about

• Apart from how they see the island, what other differences are there between Gonzalo's view of things and Antonio's and Sebastian's?

• What does Sebastian feel about the marriage and the return voyage? In what tone should he say lines 69 to 70, in your opinion?

83–84 **His word ... too**: Gonzalo's words are more powerful than the harp of Amphion. In the Greek myth his music summoned the stones to build the walls of Thebes – Gonzalo's have constructed a whole city

SEBASTIAN	With an eye of green in it.	
ANTONIO	He misses not much.	55
SEBASTIAN	No – he doth but mistake the truth totally.	
GONZALO	But the rarity of it is – which is indeed almost beyond credit –	
SEBASTIAN	As many vouched rarities are –	
GONZALO	That our garments, being, as they were, drenched in the sea, hold, notwithstanding, their freshness and glosses – being rather new-dyed than stained with salt water.	60
ANTONIO	If but one of his pockets could speak, would it not say he lies?	
SEBASTIAN	Ay, or very falsely pocket up his report.	65
GONZALO	Methinks our garments are now as fresh as when we put them on first in Africa, at the marriage of the King's fair daughter Claribel to the King of Tunis.	
SEBASTIAN	'Twas a sweet marriage – and we prosper well in our return.	70
ADRIAN	Tunis was never graced before with such a paragon to their Queen.	
GONZALO	Not since widow Dido's time.	
ANTONIO	Widow! A pox o'that! How came that widow in? Widow Dido!	75
SEBASTIAN	What if he had said 'widower Aeneas' too? Good Lord, how you take it!	
ADRIAN	'Widow Dido' said you? You make me study of that. She was of Carthage, not of Tunis.	
GONZALO	This Tunis sir, *was* Carthage.	80
ADRIAN	Carthage?	
GONZALO	I assure you, Carthage.	
ANTONIO	His word is more than the miraculous harp.	
SEBASTIAN	He hath raised the wall, and houses too!	

Alonso is tormented by
Gonzalo's reference to his
daughter's marriage. They were
on the return journey from it
when the shipwreck happened
in which he thinks his son died.

88   **kernels**: pips

91   **in good time**: at last

96   **Bate**: Except

98   **doublet**: close-fitting jacket
99   **in a sort**: in a way / comparatively
     speaking
100 **That ... for**: Good job he added 'in a
     sort'
102–3 **cram ... sense**: i.e. I am being 'force-
      fed' these words
103 **Would**: I wish
105 **rate**: opinion

---Think about

• Gonzalo seems very
  optimistic about their
  situation. How would you
  describe Alonso's mood?
  Look at lines 102 to 109.

110 **beat ... him**: push the waves down
112–13 **breasted ... swoll'n**: swam through the
       vast waves
114 **contentious**: quarrelsome
114–15 **oared ... arms**: used his arms as paddles
116–17 **that o'er ... him**: where the cliffs, worn
       away at the base by the waves, seemed
       to bend down to help him land

ANTONIO	What impossible matter will he make easy next?

85

SEBASTIAN	I think he will carry this island home in his pocket, and give it his son for an apple.

ANTONIO	And, sowing the kernels of it in the sea, bring forth more islands.

GONZALO	Ay.

90

ANTONIO	Why, in good time.

GONZALO	(*To* ALONSO) Sir, we were talking that our garments seem now as fresh as when we were at Tunis at the marriage of your daughter, who is now Queen.

ANTONIO	And the rarest that e'er came there.

95

SEBASTIAN	Bate, I beseech you, widow Dido.

ANTONIO	O, widow Dido! Ay, widow Dido.

GONZALO	Is not, sir, my doublet as fresh as the first day I wore it? I mean, in a sort.

ANTONIO	That 'sort' was well fished for.

100

GONZALO	– When I wore it at your daughter's marriage?

ALONSO	You cram these words into mine ears against

The stomach of my sense. Would I had never
Married my daughter there! For, coming thence,
My son is lost – and, in my rate, she too,   105
Who is so far from Italy removed
I ne'er again shall see her. O thou mine heir
Of Naples and of Milan, what strange fish
Hath made his meal on thee?

FRANCISCO	Sir, he may live.

I saw him beat the surges under him,   110
And ride upon their backs. He trod the water,
Whose enmity he flung aside, and breasted
The surge most swoll'n that met him. His bold head
'Bove the contentious waves he kept, and oared
Himself with his good arms in lusty stroke   115
To the shore, that o'er his wave-worn basis bowed,
As stooping to relieve him. I not doubt
He came alive to land.

Sebastian harshly blames Alonso for Ferdinand's death, because Alonso had let his daughter marry an African. This meant that they had to make a long sea journey. Gonzalo points out that this is not the time for such words.

121   **loose**: 1 lose to; 2 let her mate with

123   **Who hath … on't**: (you) who have good cause to weep at the situation

124   **importuned**: begged

126–7   **Weighed … bow**: torn between her unwillingness to marry and her unwillingness to go against her father's wishes, Claribel did not know which side of the balance to come down on

129   **of … making**: caused by your daughter's marriage

134   **time**: suitable time

136   **chirurgeonly**: like a surgeon

Think about

• Gonzalo and Francisco are trying to comfort Alonso with hope that Ferdinand is alive. What do Sebastian's statements in lines 119 to 131 reveal about his relationship with his brother, Alonso?

139   **Had … of**: If I were colonising

140   **docks, or mallows**: i.e. weeds

142   **'Scape**: Avoid
       for want of: for lack of

ALONSO   No, no – he's gone.

SEBASTIAN   Sir, you may thank *yourself* for this great loss,
             That would not bless our Europe with your daughter,   120
             But rather loose her to an African –
             Where she, at least, is banished from your eye,
             Who hath cause to wet the grief on't.

ALONSO   Prithee, peace.

SEBASTIAN   You were kneeled to, and importuned otherwise,
             By all of us – and the fair soul herself   125
             Weighed between loathness and obedience, at
             Which end o'the beam should bow. We have lost
                your son,
             I fear, for ever. Milan and Naples have
             More widows in them of this business' making
             Than we bring men to comfort them.   130
             The fault's your own.

ALONSO   So is the dearest o'the loss!

GONZALO   My lord Sebastian,
             The truth you speak doth lack some gentleness,
             And time to speak it in. You rub the sore,
             When you should bring the plaster.

SEBASTIAN   Very well.   135

ANTONIO   And most chirurgeonly.

GONZALO   (*To* ALONSO) It is foul weather in us all, good sir,
             When you are cloudy.

SEBASTIAN   Fowl weather?

ANTONIO   Very foul.

GONZALO   Had I plantation of this isle, my lord –

ANTONIO   He'd sow it with nettle-seed.

SEBASTIAN   Or docks, or mallows.   140

GONZALO   And were the king on't, what would I do?

SEBASTIAN   'Scape being drunk for want of wine.

Gonzalo imagines what he would do if he were king of the island. He imagines a perfect kingdom where no-one would need to work.

143 **commonwealth**: nation / organisation of the country
143–4 **by contraries ... things**: do everything opposite to what is usual
144 **traffic**: trade / business
145 **admit**: permit
146 **Letters**: learning
147 **use of service**: the custom of masters employing servants
succession: inheritance
148 **Bourn ... tilth**: limits of property, enclosing private land and agriculture
152 **sovereignty**: i.e. domination by a king

154–5 **All things ... endeavour**: Nature would produce everything for everybody's use, without need to work for it
155 **felony**: crime
156 **engine**: machine used in warfare
158 **Of it own kind**: as it is in its nature to do / naturally
foison: plenty
161 **whores and knaves**: prostitutes and crooks
163 **T'excel**: to outdo
Golden Age: an imaginary period in the past when everything was perfect
'Save: God save
164 **do you mark me**: are you listening

Think about

• What do you think of Gonzalo's vision of his ideal state (lines 143 to 159)? Which aspects of it seem a good idea, and which ones are impractical, in your opinion?

166–7 **minister occasion to**: provide an opportunity for
167 **sensible**: sensitive
168 **always ... laugh**: are in the habit of laughing

GONZALO	I'the commonwealth I would by contraries
	Execute all things – for no kind of traffic
	Would I admit; no name of magistrate.	**145**
	Letters should not be known; riches, poverty,
	And use of service, none; contract, succession,
	Bourn, bound of land, tilth, vineyard, none;
	No use of metal, corn, or wine, or oil;
	No occupation; all men idle, all –	**150**
	And women too, but innocent and pure;
	No sovereignty –
SEBASTIAN	Yet he would be king on't.
ANTONIO	The latter end of his commonwealth forgets the
	beginning.
GONZALO	All things in common Nature should produce
	Without sweat or endeavour. Treason, felony,	**155**
	Sword, pike, knife, gun, or need of any engine,
	Would I not have – but Nature should bring forth,
	Of it own kind, all foison, all abundance,
	To feed my innocent people.
SEBASTIAN	No marrying 'mong his subjects?	**160**
ANTONIO	None, man – all idle: whores and knaves.
GONZALO	I would with such perfection govern, sir,
	T'excel the Golden Age.
SEBASTIAN	'Save his Majesty!
ANTONIO	Long live Gonzalo!
GONZALO	And – do you mark me, sir?
ALONSO	Prithee, no more. Thou dost talk nothing to me.	**165**
GONZALO	I do well believe your Highness – and did it to minister occasion to these gentlemen, who are of such sensible and nimble lungs that they always use to laugh at nothing.
ANTONIO	'Twas you we laughed at.	**170**
GONZALO	Who in this kind of merry fooling am nothing to you. So you may continue, and laugh at nothing still.

The invisible Ariel puts a spell on all except Sebastian and Antonio to make them fall asleep.

174 **flat-long**: i.e. ineffective, because it fell with the flat of the sword, rather than the blade

175 **mettle**: spirit

175–7 **You would lift … changing**: You are all talk (lifting the moon out of its orbit is clearly impossible)

178 **a-bat-fowling**: catching birds by moonlight

180 **I warrant you**: I promise you

180–1 **adventure … weakly**: risk losing my calmness for so weak a reason as you give me

181 **heavy**: drowsy

183–4 **I wish … thoughts**: I wish shutting my eyes could shut out my thoughts

186 **omit**: ignore

187–8 **It seldom … comforter**: Sad people rarely sleep. When sleep does come to them, it is a great comfort

190 **Wondrous heavy**: I am amazingly tired

Think about

• Why do Sebastian and Antonio constantly mock Gonzalo throughout this scene?

• Who finally gets the better of the exchanges, in your opinion?

ANTONIO   What a blow was there given!

SEBASTIAN   An it had not fallen flat-long.

GONZALO   You are gentlemen of brave mettle. You would lift the   175
               moon out of her sphere, if she would continue in it five
               weeks without changing.

               Enter ARIEL *(invisible to all), playing solemn music.*

SEBASTIAN   We would so, and then go a-bat-fowling.

ANTONIO   Nay, good my lord, be not angry.

GONZALO   No, I warrant you. I will not adventure my discretion so   180
               weakly. Will you laugh me asleep, for I am very heavy?

ANTONIO   Go sleep, and hear us.

               All – except ALONSO, SEBASTIAN, *and* ANTONIO *– fall quickly
               asleep under the influence of* ARIEL'S *magic.*

ALONSO   What, all so soon asleep! I wish mine eyes
               Would, with themselves, shut up my thoughts. I find
               They are inclined to do so.

SEBASTIAN   Please you, sir,   185
               Do not omit the heavy offer of it.
               It seldom visits sorrow. When it doth,
               It is a comforter.

ANTONIO   We two, my lord,
               Will guard your person while you take your rest,
               And watch your safety.

ALONSO   Thank you. – Wondrous heavy!   190

               ALONSO *falls asleep.*

               Exit ARIEL.

SEBASTIAN   What a strange drowsiness possesses them!

ANTONIO   It is the quality o'the climate.

SEBASTIAN   Why
               Doth it not then *our* eyelids sink? I find not
               Myself disposed to sleep.

Antonio begins to try to tempt Sebastian to kill Alonso while he sleeps so that he can take his place as King of Naples.

194 my ... nimble: I feel alert

195 as: as if

196 as by a thunder-stroke: as if struck by lightning

199 Th'occasion speaks thee: This is your opportunity – take it!

201 waking: awake

203–4 It is ... sleep: you are saying the kinds of things people say in their sleep

208–9 wink'st ... waking: you are shutting your eyes to this opportunity even though you are awake

209 distinctly: meaningfully

212 if heed me: if you will listen to me

213 Trebles thee o'er: makes you three times greater than you are
standing water: i.e. indecisive, going neither forward nor back

214 To ebb: 1 to go out, like the tide; 2 to retreat / not take a chance

214–15 To ebb ... me: I am influenced by my natural laziness

216–17 you ... mock it: you really want to act even though you make a joke of it

218 more invest it: i.e. the more dress you it up

219 near ... run: i.e. they stand more chance of running aground

---

Think about

• What is the effect of the different types of imagery in this scene, for instance Sebastian's use of water imagery (lines 213 to 215)? Think about what sort of imagery is used in
(a) 'stripping ... invest' (lines 217 to 218); and
(b) 'Ebbing men ... run' (lines 218 to 219).

ANTONIO	Nor I – my spirits are nimble.
	They fell together all, as by consent: 195
	They dropped, as by a thunder-stroke. What might,
	Worthy Sebastian – O, what might ...? – No more –
	And yet methinks I see it in thy face,
	What thou should'st be. Th'occasion speaks thee – and
	My strong imagination sees a crown 200
	Dropping upon thy head.
SEBASTIAN	What, art thou waking?
ANTONIO	Do you not hear me speak?
SEBASTIAN	I do – and surely
	It is a sleepy language, and thou speak'st
	Out of thy sleep. What is it thou didst say?
	This is a strange repose, to be asleep 205
	With eyes wide open: standing, speaking, moving,
	And yet so fast asleep.
ANTONIO	Noble Sebastian,
	Thou let'st thy fortune sleep – die, rather: wink'st
	Whiles thou art waking.
SEBASTIAN	Thou dost snore distinctly:
	There's meaning in thy snores. 210
ANTONIO	I am more serious than my custom. You
	Must be so too, if heed me – which to do
	Trebles thee o'er.
SEBASTIAN	Well, I am standing water.
ANTONIO	I'll teach you how to flow.
SEBASTIAN	Do so. To ebb
	Hereditary sloth instructs me.
ANTONIO	O, – 215
	If you but knew how you the purpose cherish
	Whiles thus you mock it! How, in stripping it,
	You more invest it! Ebbing men, indeed,
	Most often do so near the bottom run
	By their own fear or sloth.

Antonio argues that there would be no-one to challenge Sebastian's claim to the throne. Ferdinand is obviously drowned and Claribel, Alonso's other child, now lives in Tunis, many miles away from Naples.

221 **setting**: determined look

221–3 **proclaim ... yield**: show that there is something on your mind which is painful for you to say

224 **of weak remembrance**: with a short memory

225 **of ... memory**: as little remembered

226 **earthed**: dead and buried

227–8 **only ... persuade**: i.e. a mere advisor

232 **that way**: i.e. that Ferdinand has survived

233–5 **even ... there**: however ambitious you might be, you could not glimpse clearly what lies ahead

235 **grant**: agree

---Think about---

- Antonio says that they had all been swallowed by the sea and then 'cast again' (line 243), which means 'cast up on land' or even 'vomited'. What else can 'cast again' mean in modern English? Look at the lines which follow, in which he uses the words 'perform ... act ... prologue'.

- What is the effect of using this language to describe the experience that Antonio and the others are having?

239 **Ten ... life**: farther than you could travel in a lifetime

240 **note**: news
post: messenger

241–2 **till ... razorable**: until babies born today become adults and start to shave

242 **from**: coming away from

243 **cast again**: cast ashore

245 **prologue**: introductory speech in a play

246 **yours ... discharge**: for you and me to perform

SEBASTIAN	Prithee, say on. 220
	The setting of thine eye and cheek proclaim
	A matter from thee; and a birth, indeed,
	Which throes thee much to yield.
ANTONIO	Thus sir:
	Although this lord of weak remembrance, this,
	Who shall be of as little memory 225
	When he is earthed, hath here almost persuaded –
	(For he's a spirit of persuasion, only
	Professes to persuade) – the King his son's alive,
	'Tis as impossible that he's undrowned
	As he that sleeps here swims.
SEBASTIAN	I have no hope 230
	That he's undrowned.
ANTONIO	O, out of that 'no hope'
	What great hope have you! No hope that way is
	Another way so high a hope, that even
	Ambition cannot pierce a wink beyond,
	But doubt discovery there. Will you grant with me 235
	That Ferdinand is drowned?
SEBASTIAN	He's gone.
ANTONIO	Then tell me,
	Who's the next heir of Naples?
SEBASTIAN	Claribel.
ANTONIO	She that is Queen of Tunis. She that dwells
	Ten leagues beyond man's life; she that from Naples
	Can have no note, unless the sun were post – 240
	The man i'the moon's too slow – till new-born chins
	Be rough and razorable; she that from whom
	We all were sea-swallowed, though some cast again –
	And that by destiny, to perform an act
	Whereof what's past is prologue: what to come, 245
	In yours and my discharge.
SEBASTIAN	What stuff is this? How say you?
	'Tis true, my brother's daughter's Queen of Tunis.
	So is she heir of Naples – 'twixt which regions
	There is some space.

Antonio encourages Sebastian
to help him kill Alonso with the
thought that, if they kill
Gonzalo as well, the remaining
lords will willingly follow a new
king.

Think about

• What arguments does
Antonio use to persuade
Sebastian to help him kill
Alonso? Look at lines 196
to 282.

• What do you learn about
Antonio and Sebastian in
this scene?

• How much persuading do
you think Sebastian needs?
Has he already decided to
kill his brother or does it
take Antonio to convince
him?

249 **cubit**: about fifty centimetres

251 **Measure us back**: know of our journey
back

252 **wake**: i.e. wake up to his fortune

253 **were no worse**: would be no worse off

254 **that**: people who

255–6 **prate ... amply**: chatter on as much

257–8 **make ... chat**: train a jackdaw to speak
as sensibly

261–2 **And ... fortune?**: So what feelings do
you have about the lucky situation you
are in?

265 **feater**: more gracefully

268 **kibe**: foot sore

269 **put ... slipper**: cause me to wear
slippers, i.e. his conscience pains him
less than a sore foot might

270 **deity**: god-like conscience

271 **candied**: 1 frozen; 2 sugared

272 **ere they molest**: before they trouble me

276 **doing thus**: i.e. stabbing him

277 **perpetual wink**: everlasting sleep
for aye: forever

278 **Sir Prudence**: Mr Careful (an insult)
i.e. Gonzalo

279 **upbraid**: criticise

280 **take suggestion**: be as easily persuaded

281–2 **tell ... hour**: agree with us that the time
is right for whatever we want to do

ANTONIO	A space whose every cubit
	Seems to cry out, 'How shall that Claribel 250
	Measure us back to Naples? Keep in Tunis,
	And let Sebastian wake!' Say this were death
	That now hath seized them: why, they were no worse
	Than now they are. There be that can rule Naples
	As well as he that sleeps; lords that can prate 255
	As amply and unnecessarily
	As this Gonzalo. I myself could make
	A chough of as deep chat. O, that you bore
	The mind that I do! What a sleep were this
	For your advancement! Do you understand me? 260

SEBASTIAN   Methinks I do.

ANTONIO   And how does your content
Tender your own good fortune?

SEBASTIAN   I remember
You did supplant your brother Prospero.

ANTONIO   True:
And look how well my garments sit upon me –
Much feater than before. My brother's servants   265
Were then my fellows: now they are my men.

SEBASTIAN   But for your conscience?

ANTONIO   Ay, sir: where lies that? If 'twere a kibe,
'Twould put me to my slipper. But I feel not
This deity in my bosom. Twenty consciences,   270
That stand 'twixt me and Milan, candied be they
And melt, ere they molest! Here lies your brother –
No better than the earth he lies upon,
If he were that which now he's like, that's dead –
Whom I, with this obedient steel, three inches of it,   275
Can lay to bed for ever. Whiles you, doing thus,
To the perpetual wink for aye might put
This ancient morsel, this Sir Prudence, who
Should not upbraid our course. For all the rest,
They'll take suggestion as a cat laps milk.   280
They'll tell the clock to any business that
We say befits the hour.

Sebastian is persuaded by the
fact that Antonio once
successfully supplanted
Prospero, and they prepare to
kill Alonso and Gonzalo.
However, as they draw their
swords, Ariel makes the King
and the others wake up.

285 tribute: the yearly sum of money that
Sebastian agreed to pay in return for
Alonso's help

291 else ... dies: otherwise his plan will
fail

293 Open-eyed: wide-awake (wordplay: 1
blatant; 2 with eyes open)
294 time: opportunity

298 sudden: quick

301 ghastly looking: 1 terrible expressions;
2 frightened look
302 securing your repose: guarding you as
you rested

---Think about ---

• Why, having been
instructed in what to do by
Antonio, does Sebastian say
'O, but one word' (line
288)? Think about (a) what
he might want to say or ask
and (b) the use of the delay
in staging the scene.

• How would you stage this
scene to show that Ariel is
invisible? Think about
where you would place
Ariel and how the spirit
should move and behave.

SEBASTIAN	Thy case, dear friend,
	Shall be my precedent: as thou got'st Milan,
	I'll come by Naples. Draw thy sword. One stroke
	Shall free thee from the tribute which thou payest; 285
	And I the King shall love thee.

ANTONIO   Draw together.
And when I rear my hand, do you the like,
To fall it on Gonzalo.

SEBASTIAN   O, but one word. (*He whispers to* ANTONIO.)

Re-enter ARIEL *(invisible), again with music.*

ARIEL   (*Standing over the sleeping* GONZALO)
My master through his Art foresees the danger
That you, his friend, are in; and sends me forth –   290
For else his project dies – to keep them living.
(*Sings in* GONZALO'S *ear*)

While you here do snoring lie,
Open-eyed Conspiracy
    His time doth take.
If of life you keep a care,   295
Shake off slumber, and beware.
    Awake, Awake!

ANTONIO   – Then let us both be sudden. (ANTONIO *and* SEBASTIAN
               draw their swords.)

GONZALO   (*Waking*) Now, good angels
Preserve the King! (*The others wake.*)

ALONSO   Why, how now? Ho, awake? (*To* SEBASTIAN *and*
               ANTONIO) Why are you drawn?   300
Wherefore this ghastly looking? What's the matter?

SEBASTIAN   Whiles we stood here securing your repose,
Even now, we heard a hollow burst of bellowing
Like bulls, or rather lions. Did't not wake you?
It struck mine ear most terribly.

ALONSO   I heard nothing.   305

Sebastian and Antonio claim that they drew their swords because they heard threatening animal noises. They all go off in search of Ferdinand.

311 **cried**: called out

313 **verily**: true

Think about

- If you were the director, how would you ask Alonso and Gonzalo to act when they wake up suddenly? Think about whether each of them would be suspicious or whether they would be convinced by Sebastian and Antonio's excuses.

ANTONIO   O, 'twas a din to fright a monster's ear,
To make an earthquake! Sure, it was the roar
Of a whole herd of lions.

ALONSO   Heard you this, Gonzalo?

GONZALO   Upon mine honour, sir, I heard a humming,
And that a strange one too, which did awake me.   **310**
I shaked you, sir, and cried. As mine eyes opened,
I saw their weapons drawn. There was a noise,
That's verily. 'Tis best we stand upon our guard,
Or that we quit this place. Let's draw our weapons.

     GONZALO *and others draw their swords.*

ALONSO   Lead off this ground – and let's make further search   **315**
For my poor son.

GONZALO   Heavens keep him from these beasts!
For he is, sure, i'the island.

ALONSO   Lead away.

ARIEL   (*Aside*) Prospero my lord shall know what I have done.
So, King, go safely on to seek thy son.

                                Exeunt.

ACT 2 SCENE 2

In this scene ...

- Stephano, the King's butler, thinks he has found a four-legged monster when he finds Trinculo, the jester, and Caliban, hiding under the same cloak.
- Caliban starts to worship Stephano as a god after he has tasted the strong wine in his bottle, and promises to show them where to find fresh water and food.
- They go off singing, Stephano believing that they are now the rulers of the island and Caliban celebrating that he has a new master.

Caliban curses Prospero for the torments he inflicts on him. Trinculo (King Alonso's jester) enters. Caliban hides under his cloak. Trinculo sees the 'monster' (Caliban) and thinks how much money he could make by putting him on show.

3 **By inch-meal**: inch by inch
4 **nor**: neither
5 **urchin-shows**: visions of spirits or goblins like hedgehogs
  pitch ... mire: throw me in the bog / marsh
6 **firebrand**: will o' the wisp (flickering lights seen on marshes)
8 **trifle**: minor misdeed
9 **mow**: make faces
11–12 **mount ... pricks**: make their prickles stand on end
13 **cloven**: forked

17 **Perchance**: Perhaps
  mind: take any notice of

18 **bear off**: protect me against

20 **Yond**: i.e. over there
21 **bombard**: big leather bottle

26 **Poor-John**: cheap dried fish
28 **painted**: i.e. shown on an advertisement
28–9 **not a ... silver**: every idiot on his day off work would pay to see the 'monster'
30 **make a man**: make a person's fortune

---Think about---
- What kinds of punishment does Prospero inflict on Caliban? Is he right to treat him as he does?

- What possible clues are there in Trinculo's speech (lines 18 to 40) about Caliban's appearance?

Another part of the island.

Enter CALIBAN *with a load of wood. A noise of thunder.*

CALIBAN   All the infections that the sun sucks up
                 From bogs, fens, flats, on Prosper fall, and make him
                 By inch-meal a disease! His spirits hear me,
                 And yet I needs must curse. But they'll nor pinch,
                 Fright me with urchin-shows, pitch me i'the mire,   5
                 Nor lead me, like a firebrand, in the dark
                 Out of my way, unless he bid 'em. But
                 For every trifle are they set upon me –
                 Sometime like apes, that mow and chatter at me,
                 And after bite me; then like hedgehogs, which   10
                 Lie tumbling in my barefoot way, and mount
                 Their pricks at my footfall. Sometime am I
                 All wound with adders, who with cloven tongues
                 Do hiss me into madness –

Enter TRINCULO (*King Alonso's jester*).

                                     – Lo, now, lo!
                 Here comes a spirit of his, and to torment me   15
                 For bringing wood in slowly. I'll fall flat.
                 Perchance he will not mind me.

CALIBAN *lies down flat under his rough cloak.*

TRINCULO   Here's neither bush nor shrub, to bear off any weather
                 at all, and another storm brewing. I hear it sing i'the
                 wind. Yond same black cloud, yond huge one, looks   20
                 like a foul bombard that would shed his liquor. If it
                 should thunder as it did before, I know not where to
                 hide my head. Yond same cloud cannot choose but fall
                 by pailfuls. What have we here? A man or a fish? Dead
                 or alive? A fish. He smells like a fish: a very ancient and 25
                 fish-like smell – a kind of, not-of-the-newest Poor-John.
                 A strange fish! Were I in England now, as once I was,
                 and had but this fish painted, not a holiday fool there
                 but would give a piece of silver: there would this
                 monster make a man. Any strange beast there makes a   30

Trinculo takes shelter under the cloak because he thinks the storm is coming again.
Stephano (the King's butler) enters, drinking and singing. He sees the cloak with the two men under it and drunkenly assumes he has found a monster with four legs.

31 **doit**: almost worthless coin

34 **hold it**: hold it back

38 **gaberdine**: cloak

40 **shroud**: cover myself
   dregs: last drops

43 **scurvy**: bad
44 **comfort**: i.e. his bottle (which comforts him)

45 **swabber**: seaman who washes the deck

51 **savour**: smell

Think about

- If you were the director, how would you bring out the visual comedy in this scene with Stephano and Trinculo?

- At the beginning of this scene (up to line 40) Caliban speaks in verse while Stephano and Trinculo speak in prose. What effect does this have?

59 **proper**: handsome
59–60 **As ... ground**: this is Stephano's drunken version of a well-known saying

man. When they will not give a doit to relieve a lame
beggar, they will lay out ten to see a dead Indian.
Legged like a man! And his fins like arms! Warm, o'my
troth! I do now let loose my opinion, hold it no longer:
this is no fish, but an islander, that hath lately suffered   35
by a thunderbolt. (*Sound of thunder again.*) Alas, the
storm is come again! My best way is to creep under his
gaberdine. There is no other shelter hereabout. Misery
acquaints a man with strange bedfellows. I will here
shroud till the dregs of the storm be past.   40

TRINCULO *hides under* CALIBAN's *cloak.*

Enter STEPHANO *(King Alonso's butler), carrying a bottle and
singing.*

STEPHANO   I shall no more to sea, to sea,
    Here shall I die ashore –

This is a very scurvy tune to sing at a man's funeral.
Well, here's my comfort.

He drinks, and sings again.

    The master, the swabber, the boatswain and I,   45
    The gunner and his mate,
Loved Mall, Meg and Marian, and Margery,
    But none of us cared for Kate.
    For she had a tongue with a tang,
    Would cry to a sailor, Go hang!   50
She loved not the savour of tar nor of pitch –
Yet a tailor might scratch her where'er she did itch.
    Then to sea, boys, and let her go hang!
This is a scurvy tune too. But here's my comfort.
(*Drinks.*)

CALIBAN   (*From under his cloak.*) Do not torment me! O!   55

STEPHANO   What's the matter? Have we devils here? Do you put
tricks upon's with savages and men of India, ha? I have
not 'scaped drowning to be afeared now of your four
legs. For it hath been said, 'As proper a man as ever went
on four legs cannot make him give ground.' And it shall   60
be said so again, while Stephano breathes at's nostrils.

Stephano gives Caliban some of his strong wine. When he hears Trinculo's voice coming from under the cloak as well, he fears that he has encountered a devil.

64 **ague**: fever

66 **but for that**: i.e. if only because he knows our language
    recover him: cure him
68 **neat's-leather**: cowhide
69 **prithee**: please

71 **after the wisest**: sensibly

74–5 **I will … him**: no sum I could sell him for could be too much
75–6 **He shall … soundly**: Whoever buys him will pay a great deal
77 **anon**: straightaway

79 **Come … ways**: Come here

83 **chaps**: jaws

88 **delicate**: clever

90 **detract**: speak insults

Think about

- Why are Trinculo and Stephano initially interested in the 'monster'? Looking at lines 27 to 32, and 66 to 76, think about how he might be of use to them.

96–7 **long spoon**: He refers to the proverb 'Whoever eats with the devil must have a long spoon'

CALIBAN	The spirit torments me! O!
STEPHANO	This is some monster of the isle with four legs, who hath got, as I take it, an ague. Where the devil should he learn our language? I will give him some relief, if it be 65 but for that. If I can recover him, and keep him tame, and get to Naples with him, he's a present for any emperor that ever trod on neat's-leather.
CALIBAN	Do not torment me, prithee! I'll bring my wood home faster. 70
STEPHANO	He's in his fit now, and does not talk after the wisest. He shall taste of my bottle. If he have never drunk wine afore, it will go near to remove his fit. If I can recover him, and keep him tame, I will not take too much for him. He shall pay for him that hath him and that 75 soundly.
CALIBAN	Thou dost me yet but little hurt. Thou wilt anon – I know it by thy trembling. Now Prosper works upon thee.
STEPHANO	Come on your ways. Open your mouth. Here is that which will give language to you, cat. Open your mouth; 80 this will shake your shaking, I can tell you, and that soundly. (*Gives a drink to* CALIBAN, *who spits it out.*) You cannot tell who's your friend. Open your chaps again.
TRINCULO	(*From the other end of* CALIBAN's *cloak.*) I should 85 know that voice. It should be – but he is drowned – and these are devils! O defend me!
STEPHANO	Four legs and two voices! A most delicate monster! His forward voice, now, is to speak well of his friend. His backward voice is to utter foul speeches and to detract. 90 If all the wine in my bottle will recover him, I will help his ague. Come! (CALIBAN *drinks again.*) Amen! I will pour some in thy other mouth.
TRINCULO	Stephano!
STEPHANO	Doth thy other mouth call me? Mercy, mercy! This is a 95 devil, and no monster! I will leave him: I have no long spoon.

Trinculo comes out from under the cloak and he and Stephano greet each other. Caliban worships Stephano as a god.

102 **very**: the real
103 **siege**: excrement
      moon-calf: monster
104 **vent**: excrete

107 **overblown**: blown over / finished

109 **Neapolitans**: people from Naples

111–12 **not constant**: unsettled

113 **an if**: if
      sprites: spirits

116 **How … hither?**: How did you get here?
118 **butt of sack**: barrel of Spanish wine

---Think about------------------

• Why does Caliban take Stephano for a god (line 114)?

• Caliban calls Stephano a 'brave' god. Look out for other instances where 'brave' (meaning fine, splendid, impressive …) is used in this play, sometimes ironically.

126 **kiss the book**: i.e. the bottle has become his holy book, to swear by
127 **made … goose**: i.e. stupid and fat

TRINCULO	Stephano! If thou beest Stephano, touch me, and speak to me: for I am Trinculo – be not afeared – thy good friend Trinculo!
STEPHANO	If thou beest Trinculo, come forth. I'll pull thee by the lesser legs. If any be Trinculo's legs, these are they. (*He pulls* TRINCULO *out.*) Thou art very Trinculo indeed! How cam'st thou to be the siege of this moon-calf? Can he vent Trinculos?
TRINCULO	I took him to be killed with a thunder-stroke. But art thou not drowned, Stephano? I hope, now, thou art not drowned. Is the storm over-blown? I hid me under the dead moon-calf's gaberdine for fear of the storm. And art thou living, Stephano? O Stephano, two Neapolitans 'scaped!
STEPHANO	Prithee, do not turn me about: my stomach is not constant.
CALIBAN	(*Aside*) These be fine things, an if they be not sprites. That's a brave god, and bears celestial liquor. I will kneel to him.
STEPHANO	How didst thou scape? How cam'st thou hither? Swear, by this bottle, how thou cam'st hither. I escaped upon a butt of sack, which the sailors heaved o'erboard, by this bottle! – which I made of the bark of a tree with mine own hands, since I was cast ashore.
CALIBAN	(*Kneeling*) I'll swear, upon that bottle, to be thy true subject; for the liquor is not earthly.
STEPHANO	Here. Swear, then, how thou escapedst.
TRINCULO	Swum ashore, man, like a duck. I can swim like a duck, I'll be sworn.
STEPHANO	Here, kiss the book. (TRINCULO *drinks.*) Though thou canst swim like a duck, thou art made like a goose.
TRINCULO	O Stephano, hast any more of this?
STEPHANO	The whole butt, man. My cellar is in a rock by the sea-side, where my wine is hid. (*To* CALIBAN) How now, moon-calf! How does thine ague?

100

105

110

115

120

125

130

Stephano convinces Caliban
that he is the man in the moon,
and Trinculo laughs at Caliban's
stupidity for believing it.
Caliban promises to show them
where to find food and drink on
the island.

134 when time was: once upon a time

136 dog ... bush: the man in the moon was
said to have a dog and a thorn-bush

139 shallow: unintelligent

141 credulous: i.e. he believes that
Stephano is the man in the moon
Well drawn: i.e. that's a good long
drink you've taken
142 in good sooth: truly
145 perfidious: treacherous / disloyal

149 puppy-headed: stupid

153 But ... drink: Except that the monster's
drunk

Think about

• In what ways is Caliban's
behaviour here different
from what we have seen
earlier?

• Why does Trinculo dislike
Caliban? What criticisms
does he have of the
'monster'?

CALIBAN	Hast thou not dropped from heaven?
STEPHANO	Out o'the moon, I do assure thee. I was the man i'the moon when time was.
CALIBAN	I have seen thee in her, and I do adore thee. My 135 mistress showed me thee, and thy dog, and thy bush.
STEPHANO	Come, swear to that: kiss the book. I will furnish it anon with new contents. Swear.

CALIBAN *drinks again.*

TRINCULO	By this good light, this is a very shallow monster! I afeared of him? A very weak monster! The man i'the 140 moon! A most poor credulous monster! Well drawn, monster, in good sooth!
CALIBAN	I'll show thee every fertile inch o'the island; and I will kiss thy foot. I prithee, be my god.
TRINCULO	By this light, a most perfidious and drunken monster! 145 When his god's asleep, he'll rob his bottle.
CALIBAN	I'll kiss thy foot. I'll swear myself thy subject.
STEPHANO	Come on, then. Down, and swear.
TRINCULO	I shall laugh myself to death at this puppy-headed monster. A most scurvy monster! I could find in my 150 heart to beat him –
STEPHANO	Come, kiss.
TRINCULO	– But that the poor monster's in drink. An abominable monster!
CALIBAN	I'll show thee the best springs. I'll pluck thee berries. 155 I'll fish for thee, and get thee wood enough. A plague upon the tyrant that I serve! I'll bear him no more sticks, but follow thee, Thou wondrous man.
TRINCULO	(*Aside*) A most ridiculous monster, to make a wonder of 160 a poor drunkard!

Stephano, Trinculo, and Caliban go off, with Caliban singing. Stephano claims that they are now the rulers of the island. Caliban celebrates his freedom from Prospero.

162 crabs: probably crab-apples
163 pig-nuts: edible roots growing underground
165 marmoset: small monkey
166 filberts: hazelnuts
167 scamels: probably sea-birds

175 firing: firewood

177 trenchering: wooden plates

179 Get … man: i.e. Prospero will have to find a new servant
180 high-day!: holiday!

182 brave: fine / splendid

Think about

• What does Stephano's remark in lines 169 to 170 remind you of? What earlier example of 'inheriting' the island have we heard about? Look back at Act 1 Scene 2, lines 332 to 345.

• Why might audiences in Shakespeare's time have been interested in the idea of Europeans 'inheriting' the lands they came across in their voyages around the world?

CALIBAN	I prithee, let me bring thee where crabs grow –
	And I with my long nails will dig thee pig-nuts,
	Show thee a jay's nest, and instruct thee how
	To snare the nimble marmoset. I'll bring thee **165**
	To clustering filberts, and sometimes I'll get thee
	Young scamels from the rock. Wilt thou go with me?
STEPHANO	I prithee now, lead the way, without any more talking.
	Trinculo, the King and all our company else being
	drowned, *we* will inherit here. Here, bear my bottle. **170**
	Fellow Trinculo, we'll fill him by and by again.
CALIBAN	(*Sings drunkenly*) Farewell, master! Farewell, farewell!
TRINCULO	A howling monster! A drunken monster!
CALIBAN	(*Singing and shouting*)
	No more dams I'll make for fish,
	Nor fetch in firing **175**
	At requiring,
	Nor scrape trenchering, nor wash dish!
	'Ban! 'Ban! Ca–Caliban! –
	Has a new master – Get a new man!
	Freedom, high-day! High-day, freedom! Freedom, **180**
	high-day, freedom!
STEPHANO	O brave monster! Lead the way.

Exeunt.

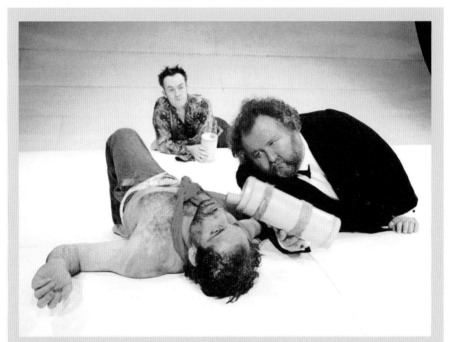

RSC, 2000

RSC, 1982

RSC, 1998

RSC, 1988

In this scene ...

- Prospero has set Ferdinand the task of carrying logs, which he is happy to do as long as he can see Miranda.
- Miranda tells Ferdinand her name. They declare their love for one another and she offers to marry him.
- Ferdinand offers to be Miranda's husband, much to the delight of Prospero, who has been secretly watching.
- Prospero returns to his magic books as he still has much to accomplish.

Made into a slave by Prospero, Ferdinand is now carrying logs. Though Miranda feels sorry for him, he is willing to do the work.

1–2 **their labour ... off**: pleasure cancels out the pain

2 **baseness**: degrading activity

4 **mean**: humble

5 **odious**: hateful

6 **quickens**: brings to life

8 **crabbed**: bad-tempered

11 **Upon ... injunction**: following his harsh command

13 **Had ... executor**: never had such a noble person carry it out

15 **Most ... it**: most strongly when I am working hardest

16 **would**: wish

17 **enjoined**: ordered

19 **'Twill weep**: i.e. it will seem to give off tears

22 **discharge**: carry out

Think about

- How are the conflicting reactions Ferdinand is experiencing reflected in his language? Think about the contrast in his feelings about finding Miranda and having to serve Prospero.

In front of Prospero's cave.

Enter FERDINAND, carrying a log.

FERDINAND   *(Putting down the log)* There be some sports are
                 painful, and their labour
             Delight in them sets off. Some kinds of baseness
             Are nobly undergone, and most poor matters
             Point to rich ends. This my mean task
             Would be as heavy to me as odious, but   5
             The mistress which I serve quickens what's dead,
             And makes my labours pleasures. O, she is
             Ten times more gentle than her father's crabbed –
             And he's composed of harshness! I must remove
             Some thousands of these logs, and pile them up,   10
             Upon a sore injunction. My sweet mistress
             Weeps when she sees me work, and says such baseness
             Had never like executor. I forget –
             (He picks up the log again)
             – But these sweet thoughts do even refresh my labours,
             Most busiest, when I do it.

*Enter MIRANDA – and PROSPERO, who watches from a distance,
unseen.*

MIRANDA   Alas now, pray you   15
             Work not so hard! I would the lightning had
             Burnt up those logs that you are enjoined to pile!
             Pray, set it down, and rest you. When this burns,
             'Twill weep for having wearied you. My father
             Is hard at study. Pray, now, rest yourself.   20
             He's safe for these three hours.

FERDINAND   O most dear mistress,
             The sun will set before I shall discharge
             What I must strive to do.

MIRANDA   If you'll sit down.
             I'll bear your logs the while. Pray give me that:
             I'll carry it to the pile.

Against her father's wishes, Miranda tells Ferdinand her name, and they express their happiness at having met one another.

Think about

- Miranda's name and the word 'admiration' both come from a Latin word meaning 'wonder'. In what ways is her behaviour reflected in her name?

26 **crack my sinews**: strain my muscles and tendons

28 **become**: suit

30 **my … to it**: I do it willingly

31 **infected**: i.e. she has fallen in love
32 **visitation**: attack of the plague

34 **beseech**: beg

37 **hest**: command
  Miranda: the name comes from a Latin word meaning 'wonder'

39 **Full many a lady**: Many women
40 **eyed … regard**: gazed at with greatest approval
41–2 **hath … ear**: has captivated me as I listened
42 **several**: particular
45 **Did … owed**: contrasted with the finest qualities she possessed
46 **put … foil**: defeated it
47 **peerless**: without equal

50 **Save … own**: except my own, which I have seen in the mirror
52–3 **How … skilless of**: I have no idea what people elsewhere look like
53–4 **modesty … dower**: virginity, the most valuable possession I have, to offer at my marriage

FERDINAND	No, precious creature. 25

FERDINAND   No, precious creature.   25
I had rather crack my sinews, break my back,
Than you should such dishonour undergo,
While I sit lazy by.

MIRANDA   It would become me
As well as it does you – and I should do it
With much more ease, for my good will is to it,   30
And yours it is against.

PROSPERO   (*Aside*) Poor worm, thou art infected!
This visitation shows it.

MIRANDA   You look wearily.

FERDINAND   No, noble mistress. 'Tis fresh morning with me
When you are by at night. I do beseech you –
(***Putting down the log***) Chiefly that I might set it in my
    prayers –   35
What is your name?

MIRANDA   Miranda. O my father,
I have broke your hest to say so!

FERDINAND   Admired Miranda!
Indeed the top of admiration – worth
What's dearest to the world! Full many a lady
I have eyed with best regard, and many a time   40
The harmony of their tongues hath into bondage
Brought my too diligent ear. For several virtues
Have I liked several women – never any
With so full soul, but some defect in her
Did quarrel with the noblest grace she owed,   45
And put it to the foil. But you – o you,
So perfect and so peerless – are created
Of every creature's best!

MIRANDA   I do not know
One of my sex – no woman's face remember,
Save, from my glass, mine own. Nor have I seen   50
More that I may call men than you, good friend,
And my dear father. How features are abroad,
I am skilless of – but, by my modesty,
The jewel in my dower, I would not wish

Miranda and Ferdinand declare their love for one another. Prospero has been watching them, hidden, and quietly blesses their relationship. Miranda offers to be Ferdinand's wife.

57 prattle: chatter
58 precepts: commands

59 condition: rank in society

63 flesh-fly: fly that lays its eggs in dead flesh
blow: lay its eggs in

69 profess: declare
kind event: happy outcome
70–1 If hollowly … mischief: If I speak insincerely, may all the good things promised me turn into bad

75 grace: goodness
76 breeds: grows

79 to want: if I do not get
trifling: prattling
81 Hence … cunning: Away with clever words and shyness!

84 maid: 1 virgin; 2 servant
fellow: i.e. wife
86 will or no: want me to or not

Think about

- Miranda's offer to marry Ferdinand in line 83 seems to come very quickly. What can account for it?

- What kind of language do Miranda and Ferdinand use with one another? What does it reveal about their feelings?

Any companion in the world but you –   55
Nor can imagination form a shape,
Besides yourself, to like of. But I prattle
Something too wildly, and my father's precepts
I therein do forget.

FERDINAND   I am, in my condition,
A prince, Miranda: I do think, a King –   60
I would not so! – and would no more endure
This wooden slavery than to suffer
The flesh-fly blow my mouth. Hear my soul speak:
The very instant that I saw you, did
My heart fly to your service – there resides,   65
To make me slave to it – and for your sake
Am I this patient log-man.

MIRANDA   Do you love me?

FERDINAND   O heaven, O earth, bear witness to this sound
And crown what I profess with kind event,
If I speak true! If hollowly, invert   70
What best is boded me to mischief! I,
Beyond all limit of what else i'the world,
Do love, prize, honour you.

MIRANDA   I am a fool
To weep at what I am glad of.

PROSPERO   (*Aside*) Fair encounter
Of two most rare affections! Heavens rain grace   75
On that which breeds between 'em!

FERDINAND   Wherefore weep you?

MIRANDA   At mine unworthiness, that dare not offer
What I desire to give; and much less take
What I shall die to want. But this is trifling –
And all the more it seeks to hide itself,   80
The bigger bulk it shows. Hence, bashful cunning!
And prompt me, plain and holy innocence!
I am your wife if you will marry me:
If not, I'll die your maid. To be your fellow
You may deny me; but I'll be your servant,   85
Whether you will or no.

Ferdinand kneels in front of Miranda and offers to be her husband. Still hidden, Prospero rejoices. He returns to his magic book as he still has much to do before supper.

89   **As bondage ... freedom**: as ever the slave is to be free

91   **A thousand ... !**: i.e. farewells

95   **ere**: before
96   **appertaining**: to do with this

Think about

- In lines 92 to 94, Prospero says that he cannot be as delighted as Miranda and Ferdinand because he is not surprised by what has happened. Why is he not surprised?

FERDINAND   My mistress, dearest,
              (*He kneels*) And I thus humble ever.

MIRANDA   My husband, then?

FERDINAND   Ay, with a heart as willing
              As bondage e'er of freedom! Here's my hand.

MIRANDA   And mine, with my heart in't. And now farewell   90
              Till half an hour hence.

FERDINAND   A thousand thousand!

              Exit MIRANDA. *Exit* FERDINAND*, separately, carrying the log.*

PROSPERO   So glad of this as they I cannot be,
              Who are surprised with all – but my rejoicing
              At nothing can be more. I'll to my book –
              For yet, ere supper-time, must I perform   95
              Much business appertaining.

                                                      Exit.

In this scene ...

- Caliban tells Stephano and Trinculo about Prospero. He claims that Prospero stole the island from him.
- Caliban encourages them to kill Prospero, and Stephano agrees.
- Ariel overhears their conversation and goes off to warn Prospero.

Now very drunk, Stephano and Trinculo explore the island with Caliban. Trinculo mocks the way Caliban seems to worship Stephano.

1 **butt is out**: barrel is empty
2 **bear ... 'em**: stand firm and attack, i.e. drink up!

4 **folly of**: low level of intelligence on

6 **be brained**: have brains as drunk

8 **set**: sunken, i.e. fixed, because drunk

9 **brave**: amazing
10 **set**: placed

11 **sack**: sherry (strong wine)

13 **five ... leagues**: about a hundred miles

15 **standard**: flag-carrier

16 **list**: like
   he's no standard: i.e. because he is drunk and having difficulty standing
18 **go**: walk
   lie: 1 lie down; 2 tell lies

20 **Moon-calf**: monster

Think about

- Why do you think Trinculo continues to be very critical of Caliban?

24 **in case**: in a fit state
   jostle: push around
25 **debauched**: corrupted / messed-up

29 **Lo**: Listen

Another part of the island.

Enter CALIBAN, STEPHANO, *and* TRINCULO.

STEPHANO	Tell not me! When the butt is out, we will drink water – not a drop before. Therefore bear up, and board 'em. Servant-monster, drink to me.
TRINCULO	Servant-monster! The folly of this island! They say there's but five upon this isle. We are three of them. If the other two be brained like us, the state totters!
STEPHANO	Drink, servant-monster, when I bid thee! Thy eyes are almost set in thy head.
TRINCULO	Where should they be set else? He were a brave monster indeed, if they were set in his tail.
STEPHANO	My man-monster hath drowned his tongue in sack. For my part, the sea cannot drown me. I swam, ere I could recover the shore, five-and-thirty leagues off and on. By this light, thou shalt be my lieutenant, monster, or my standard.
TRINCULO	Your lieutenant, if you list: he's no standard.
STEPHANO	We'll not run, Monsieur Monster.
TRINCULO	Nor go neither – but you'll lie like dogs, and yet say nothing neither.
STEPHANO	Moon-calf, speak once in thy life, if thou beest a good moon-calf.
CALIBAN	(*Very drunk*) How does thy honour? Let me lick thy shoe. I'll not serve *him*. He is not valiant.
TRINCULO	Thou liest, most ignorant monster! I am in case to jostle a constable. Why, thou debauched fish, thou, was there ever man a coward that hath drunk so much sack as I today? Wilt thou tell a monstrous lie, being but half a fish and half a monster?
CALIBAN	Lo, how he mocks me! Wilt thou let him, my lord?

5

10

15

20

25

Caliban tells Stephano that Prospero is a magician who stole the island from him. He promises to take Stephano to Prospero so that he can kill him while he is asleep. The invisible Ariel imitates Trinculo's voice and interrupts their conversation, calling Caliban a liar.

30 **quoth he?**: did he say?
31 **natural**: idiot
32 **prithee**: beg you

34 **mutineer**: rebel
   the next tree: i.e. you'll be hanged

37 **suit**: request

38 **Marry**: Indeed (by Mary)

45 **would**: wish

47 **in's**: in his
48 **supplant**: remove

50 **Mum**: Stay quiet

54 **this thing**: i.e. Trinculo

57 **compassed**: achieved / brought about
58 **party**: person we're talking about

Think about

• In what ways is Stephano now behaving like the ruler of the island? If he were ruler, what kind of ruler would he be?

• As a director, how would you stage the sequence in which Ariel imitates Trinculo's voice (lines 40 to 74) so as to make it both believable and funny?

TRINCULO	'Lord,' quoth he? That a monster should be such a **30** natural!
CALIBAN	Lo, lo, again! Bite him to death, I prithee.
STEPHANO	Trinculo, keep a good tongue in your head. If you prove a mutineer – the next tree! The poor monster's my subject, and he shall not suffer indignity. **35**
CALIBAN	I thank my noble lord. Wilt thou be pleased to hearken once again to the suit I made to thee?
STEPHANO	Marry, will I. Kneel and repeat it. I will stand, and so shall Trinculo.

Enter ARIEL *(invisible).*

CALIBAN	As told thee before, I am subject to a tyrant – **40** A sorcerer, that by his cunning hath cheated me Of the island.
ARIEL	Thou liest.
CALIBAN	(*To* TRINCULO) 'Thou liest,' thou jesting monkey, thou! I would my valiant master would destroy thee! **45** I do not lie.
STEPHANO	Trinculo, if you trouble him any more in's tale, by this hand, I will supplant some of your teeth.
TRINCULO	Why, I said nothing!
STEPHANO	Mum, then and no more. (*To* CALIBAN) Proceed. **50**
CALIBAN	I say, by sorcery he got this isle – From me he got it. If thy greatness will Revenge it on him – for I know *thou* dar'st, But this thing dare not –
STEPHANO	That's most certain. **55**
CALIBAN	Thou shalt be lord of it, and I'll serve thee.
STEPHANO	How now shall this be compassed? Canst thou bring me to the party?
CALIBAN	Yea, yea, my lord. I'll yield him thee asleep, Where thou may'st knock a nail into his head. **60**
ARIEL	Thou liest: thou canst not.

Stephano hits Trinculo because he believes he called Caliban a liar. Caliban gives Stephano and Trinculo suggestions about how they might kill Prospero.

62   pied ninny: stupid jester
patch: fool

65   brine: salt water
66   quick freshes: flowing fresh-water springs

69   stockfish: salted fish that had to be beaten to make it tender

73–4   As you … time: If you like this beating, just call me a liar again

75   Out … too?: Are you crazy and deaf as well?

77   murrain: plague

Think about

• What parallels can you see between Caliban's plan to kill Prospero while he is asleep, and another strand in the plot?

• Do you think that Caliban's claim about how Prospero's spirits feel about their master (lines 92 to 93) is true of Ariel? Do you think Caliban's claim that Prospero would be nothing without his books is true?

86   brain him: bash his brains out

88   paunch him: stab him in the stomach
89   wezand: windpipe / throat

91   sot: ignorant fool

93   rootedly: deeply

CALIBAN	What a pied ninny's this! (*To* TRINCULO) Thou scurvy patch! (*To* STEPHANO) I do beseech thy greatness, give him blows And take his bottle from him. When that's gone, He shall drink nought but brine – for I'll not show him 65 Where the quick freshes are.
STEPHANO	Trinculo, run into no further danger! Interrupt the monster one word further, and, by this hand, I'll turn my mercy out o'doors, and make a stockfish of thee.
TRINCULO	Why, what did I? I did nothing! I'll go farther off. 70
STEPHANO	Didst thou not say he lied?
ARIEL	Thou liest.
STEPHANO	Do I so? Take thou that! (*He hits* TRINCULO.) As you like this, give me the lie another time!
TRINCULO	I did not give the lie! Out o'your wits, and hearing too? 75 A pox o'your bottle! This can sack and drinking do. A murrain on your monster, and the devil take your fingers!
CALIBAN	Ha, ha, ha!
STEPHANO	(*To* CALIBAN) Now, forward with your tale. 80 (*To* TRINCULO) Prithee, stand farther off.
CALIBAN	Beat him enough. After a little time, I'll beat him too.
STEPHANO	(*To* TRINCULO) Stand farther! – (*To* CALIBAN)) Come, proceed.
CALIBAN	Why, as I told thee, 'tis a custom with him 85 I'th'afternoon to sleep. There thou may'st brain him, Having first seized his books – or with a log Batter his skull, or paunch him with a stake, Or cut his wezand with thy knife. Remember First to possess his books – for without them 90 He's but a sot, as I am, nor hath not One spirit to command. They all do hate him As rootedly as I. Burn but his books.

Caliban tells Stephano and Trinculo that Prospero has a beautiful daughter who will make Stephano a fine wife. Stephano agrees to kill Prospero. Ariel overhears their plot.

94 **brave**: impressive
   utensils: 1 tools for magic; 2 luxury household goods
95 **deck withal**: decorate it with
96 **that ... consider**: the main thing you need to keep in mind
98 **nonpareil**: woman without equal
99 **dam**: mother

101 **brave**: fine

102 **become**: be perfect for
   warrant: promise
103 **bring ... brood**: produce fine children for you

106 **viceroys**: deputy rulers

115 **jocund**: cheerful
   troll the catch: sing the song
116 **but while-ere**: just a little while ago
117 **do reason**: agree to anything reasonable

119 **Flout ... 'em**: mock them and jeer at them

s.d. **tabor**: small drum

---Think about

• Are Caliban and Miranda similar in any way? Think about what Caliban's remark about women (lines 98 to 99) reminds you of, earlier in the play.

He has brave utensils – for so he calls them –
Which, when he has a house, he'll deck withal.   95
And that most deeply to consider is
The beauty of his daughter. He himself
Calls her a nonpareil. I never saw a woman
But only Sycorax my dam and she –
But she as far surpasseth Sycorax   100
As great'st does least.

STEPHANO   Is it so brave a lass?

CALIBAN   Ay, lord. She will become thy bed, I warrant,
And bring thee forth brave brood.

STEPHANO   Monster, I will kill this man. His daughter and I will be
king and queen – save our graces! – and Trinculo and 105
thyself shall be viceroys. Dost thou like the plot,
Trinculo?

TRINCULO   Excellent.

STEPHANO   Give me thy hand. I am sorry I beat thee: but, while
thou liv'st, keep a good tongue in thy head.   110

CALIBAN   Within this half hour will he be asleep.
Wilt thou destroy him then?

STEPHANO   Ay, on mine honour!

ARIEL   (*Aside*) This will I tell my master.

CALIBAN   Thou mak'st me merry! I am full of pleasure.
Let us be jocund! Will you troll the catch   115
You taught me but while-ere?

STEPHANO   At thy request, monster, I will do reason, any reason. –
Come on, Trinculo, let us sing.
(*They sing*)
Flout 'em and scout 'em,
And scout 'em and flout 'em: 120
Thought is free.

CALIBAN   That's not the tune.

ARIEL *plays the tune on a tabor and pipe.*

STEPHANO   What is this same?

Caliban tells Stephano and Trinculo not to be afraid of the music they hear. Following the sound, he leads them off to where they can find Prospero.

124–5 **the picture of Nobody**: i.e. an invisible being

127 **take't … list**: do as you please

129 **He … debts**: If you're dead, you don't owe anybody anything

133 **airs**: tunes
134 **twangling instruments**: i.e. harps, lutes, etc.

144 **by and by**: soon
story: plan

148 **taborer**: drummer
lays it on: plays enthusiastically

---Think about---

• How does Caliban's language in lines 132 to 140 differ from the cursing and violent nature of his language earlier?

• What aspect of Caliban's character is shown here that we have not seen before?

TRINCULO	This is the tune of our catch, played by the picture of Nobody! **125**
STEPHANO	If thou beest a man, show thyself in thy likeness! If thou beest a devil, take't as thou list.
TRINCULO	Oh, forgive me my sins!
STEPHANO	He that dies pays all debts. I defy thee! Mercy upon us!
CALIBAN	Art thou afeared? **130**
STEPHANO	No, monster, not I.
CALIBAN	Be not afeared. The isle is full of noises, Sounds and sweet airs, that give delight, and hurt not. Sometimes a thousand twangling instruments Will hum about mine ears – and sometime voices, **135** That, if I then had waked after long sleep, Will make me sleep again. And then, in dreaming, The clouds methought would open, and show riches Ready to drop upon me – that, when I waked, I cried to dream again. **140**
STEPHANO	This will prove a brave kingdom to me, where I shall have my music for nothing.
CALIBAN	When Prospero is destroyed.
STEPHANO	That shall be by and by. I remember the story.
TRINCULO	The sound is going away. Let's follow it, and after do **145** our work.
STEPHANO	Lead, monster. We'll follow. I would I could see this taborer: he lays it on.
TRINCULO	Wilt come? I'll follow, Stephano.

Exeunt.

In this scene ...

- Prospero causes spirits to bring a feast to Alonso and his companions.
- Before they can eat, Ariel appears in a terrifying form and reminds Alonso, Antonio and Sebastian of their sins.

Antonio sees that Alonso is exhausted and reminds Sebastian of his pledge to kill him.

1 **By'r lakin**: By Our Lady (i.e. the Virgin Mary)
3 **forth-rights and meanders**: straight and winding paths

5 **attached with**: gripped by
6 **dulling**: lowering
7–8 **Even ... flatterer**: i.e. I will no longer fool myself that there is any hope

10 **frustrate**: fruitless

12 **for one repulse**: because of one setback
12–13 **forgo ... t'effect**: give up the plan you decided to carry out
throughly: fully

15 **oppressed**: tired out

Think about

- Some productions show Sebastian being less keen to carry out the plan than Antonio in lines 11 to 18. What evidence is there to support that interpretation?

- If you were directing the scene, how keen would your Sebastian seem to be?

Another part of the island.

Enter ALONSO, SEBASTIAN, ANTONIO, GONZALO, ADRIAN,

FRANCISCO, *and others.*

GONZALO	By'r lakin, I can go no further, sir,
	My old bones ache. Here's a maze trod, indeed,
	Through forth-rights and meanders! By your patience,
	I needs must rest me.

ALONSO   Old lord, I cannot blame thee,
Who am myself attached with weariness   5
To the dulling of my spirits. Sit down, and rest.
Even here I will put off my hope, and keep it
No longer for my flatterer. He is drowned
Whom thus we stray to find – and the sea mocks
Our frustrate search on land. Well, let him go.   10

ANTONIO   (*Aside to* SEBASTIAN) I am right glad that he's so out of
    hope.
Do not, for one repulse, forgo the purpose
That you resolved t'effect.

SEBASTIAN   (*Aside to* ANTONIO) The next advantage
We will take throughly.

ANTONIO   (*Aside to* SEBASTIAN) Let it be tonight.
For, now they are oppressed with travel, they   15
Will not, nor cannot, use such vigilance
As when they are fresh.

SEBASTIAN   (*Aside to* ANTONIO) I say, tonight. No more.

Strange and solemn music plays. Enter PROSPERO *above the
scene (invisible, in his magic cloak), looking down on King
Alonso and the others.*

ALONSO   What harmony is this? My good friends, hark!

GONZALO   Marvellous sweet music!

Spirits commanded by Prospero
bring in a table loaded with
food.

20 **keepers**: guardian angels

21 **living drollery**: puppet-show but with
live actors

23 **phoenix**: mythical bird only one of
which lived at a time

25 **what … credit**: anything else that
seems unbelievable

30 **certes**: certainly

36 **muse**: wonder at

38 **want**: lack

39 **dumb discourse**: silent conversation

Praise in departing: Don't praise it
until you have seen everything

41 **viands**: food
stomachs: appetites

Think about

- If you were a director, how
  would you represent the
  'strange Spirit-shapes' (a) on
  stage and (b) on film? Think
  about how the characters
  respond to them in lines
  20 to 40.

*Enter several strange Spirit-shapes, bringing a table with rich
food. They dance gracefully around it (with gestures greeting
King Alonso and the others, and inviting them to eat), before
departing.*

ALONSO	Give us kind keepers, heavens! – What were these?	**20**

SEBASTIAN   A living drollery! Now I will believe
That there are unicorns – that in Arabia
There is one tree, the phoenix' throne, one phoenix
At this hour reigning there.

ANTONIO   I'll believe both –
And what does else want credit, come to me,   **25**
And I'll be sworn 'tis true. Travellers ne'er did lie,
Though fools at home condemn 'em.

GONZALO   If in Naples
I should report this now, would they believe me?
If I should say, I saw such islanders? –
For, certes, these are people of the island –   **30**
Who, though they are of monstrous shape, yet note,
Their manners are more gentle, kind, than of
Our human generation you shall find
Many – nay, almost any.

PROSPERO   (*Aside*) Honest lord,
Thou hast said well – for some of you there present   **35**
Are worse than devils.

ALONSO   I cannot too much muse
Such shapes, such gesture, and such sound, expressing –
Although they want the use of tongue – a kind
Of excellent dumb discourse.

PROSPERO   (*Aside*) Praise in departing.

FRANCISCO   They vanished strangely.

SEBASTIAN   No matter, since   **40**
They have left their viands behind – for we have
   stomachs.
Will't please you taste of what is here?

ALONSO   Not I!

As the men are about to eat, Ariel enters in the shape of a monstrous harpy and speaks to Alonso, Antonio, and Sebastian, accusing them of their crimes.

Think about

• Line 48 refers to voyages of discovery. What other things are there in the play which remind us that Shakespeare was writing for an audience who were fascinated by travellers' tales about strange new lands and creatures?

• In line 53, Ariel says he is addressing three men. Which characters hear this speech and which don't? What do they learn about their current situation and their future?

---

44 **mountaineers**: people who live in mountains

45–6 **Dew-lapped ... flesh**: with folds of skin hanging from their necks

48 **putter-out ... one**: traveller who raised money for a voyage by promising profits to investors

49 **Good warrant**: confirmation
stand to: set to work, i.e. eating

s.d. **Harpy**: terrifying and monstrous mythical bird of prey with a woman's head

53 **three men**: i.e. Alonso, Sebastian and Antonio

53–6 **Destiny ... up you**: fate, which governs the earth, has caused the sea, which is never full, to vomit you up

59 **such-like valour**: i.e. the courage of madness

60 **proper**: own

61 **ministers**: agents

62 **tempered**: made

63 **bemocked-at**: ridiculous

65 **One dowle ... plume**: the smallest feather in my plumage

66 **like**: similarly

67 **massy**: heavy

71 **requit**: repaid (i.e. by throwing them ashore)

74 **Incensed**: stirred up to anger

76 **bereft**: deprived / robbed

77 **Ling'ring perdition**: long-lasting and complete ruin

GONZALO	Faith, sir, you need not fear. When we were boys,	
	Who would believe that there were mountaineers	
	Dew-lapped like bulls, whose throats had hanging at 'em	45
	Wallets of flesh? Or that there were such men	
	Whose heads stood in their breasts? Which now we find	
	Each putter-out of five for one will bring us	
	Good warrant of.	

ALONSO   I will stand to, and feed,
              Although my last, no matter, since I feel   50
              The best is past. Brother, my lord the Duke,
              Stand to, and do as we.

Thunder and lightning. Enter ARIEL, *like a Harpy. He claps his
wings over the table, and the food vanishes.*

ARIEL   You are three men of sin, whom Destiny –
              That hath to instrument this lower world
              And what is in't – the never-surfeited sea   55
              Hath caused to belch up you. And on this island,
              Where man doth not inhabit – you 'mongst men
              Being most unfit to live. I have made you mad.
              And even with such-like valour men hang and drown
              Their proper selves. (ALONSO, SEBASTIAN, *and* ANTONIO
                draw their swords.) You fools! I and my fellows   60
              Are ministers of Fate! The elements,
              Of whom your swords are tempered, may as well
              Wound the loud winds, or with bemocked-at stabs
              Kill the still-closing waters, as diminish
              One dowle that's in my plume. My fellow-ministers   65
              Are like invulnerable. If you *could* hurt,
              Your swords are now too massy for your strengths,
              And will not be uplifted. But remember –
              For that's my business to you – that you three
              From Milan did supplant good Prospero: 70
              Exposed unto the sea, which hath requit it,
              Him and his innocent child. For which foul deed
              The powers – delaying, not forgetting – have
              Incensed the seas and shores, yea, all the creatures,
              Against your peace. Thee of thy son, Alonso,   75
              They have bereft; and do pronounce by me
              Ling'ring perdition – worse than any death

The spirits carry away the table. Alonso, reminded by Ariel that he helped Antonio to overthrow Prospero, is struck with guilt and begins to feel desperate.

78 **attend**: accompany (i.e. from now on)
79–82 **whose wraths ... ensuing**: the only way, to avoid that which will otherwise fall upon you here in this desolate island, is to repent and lead a pure life

83 **Bravely**: Brilliantly
84 **a grace ... devouring**: it was amazingly skilful and effective (the banquet appeared to be 'devoured')
85 **bated**: left out
86–7 **with good ... strange**: in a lifelike way and with extraordinary care
87–8 **my meaner ... done**: my spirits inferior to Ariel have performed their individual roles
89–90 **knit up ... distractions**: trapped by their temporary madness

96 **billows**: waves

99 **bass my trespass**: announced my guilt in a deep voice
100 **i'the ooze**: in the mud on the sea-bed
101 **e'er plummet sounded**: any depth ever measured by a lead weight

Think about

• What hope does Ariel offer Alonso of how to avoid 'Ling'ring perdition' (line 77)?

• How do Alonso, Sebastian, and Antonio react to Ariel's speech? Why does Alonso respond differently?

103 **o'er**: all, one after another

   second: supporter

Can be at once – shall step by step attend
You and your ways – whose wraths to guard you from –
Which here, in this most desolate isle, else falls   80
Upon your heads – is nothing but heart's sorrow
And a clear life ensuing.

Thunder. ARIEL *disappears. The Spirit-shapes re-enter, and*
dance with mocking gestures, making faces. They carry away
the table.

PROSPERO   Bravely the figure of this Harpy hast thou
Performed, my Ariel: a grace it had, devouring!
Of my instruction hast thou nothing bated   85
In what thou hadst to say. So, with good life
And observation strange, my meaner ministers
Their several kinds have done. My high charms work –
And these mine enemies are all knit up
In their distractions. They now are in my power: 90
And in these fits I leave them, while I visit
Young Ferdinand – whom they suppose is drowned –
And his and mine loved darling.

                                                          Exit.

GONZALO   I'the name of something holy, sir, why stand you
In this strange stare?

ALONSO   O, it is monstrous, monstrous!   95
Methought the billows spoke, and told me of it;
The winds did sing it to me; and the thunder –
That deep and dreadful organ-pipe – pronounced
The name of Prosper. It did bass my trespass!
Therefore my son i'the ooze is bedded – and   100
I'll seek him deeper than e'er plummet sounded,
And with him there lie mudded.

                                                          Exit.

SEBASTIAN   But one fiend at a time,
I'll fight their legions o'er!

ANTONIO   I'll be thy second.

                          Exit SEBASTIAN, *with* ANTONIO.

Affected in different ways by Ariel's words, Sebastian, Antonio, and Alonso have run off. Gonzalo fears that they might come to harm.

105 **poison ... after**: delayed-action poison
106 **'gins**: begins

108 **ecstasy**: fit of madness

Think about

- Gonzalo talks about the delayed-action poison beginning to work on Alonso, Sebastian, and Antonio (lines 104 to 106). What is the nature of this 'poison'? Why has it taken time to take effect?

- What is Gonzalo's interpretation of the reactions and behaviour of Alonso, Sebastian, and Antonio?

GONZALO   All three of them are desperate. Their great guilt
            Like poison given to work a great time after,   **105**
            Now 'gins to bite the spirits. I do beseech you,
            That are of suppler joints, follow them swiftly,
            And hinder them from what this ecstasy
            May now provoke them to.

ADRIAN   (*To* GONZALO) Follow, I pray you.

                                                    Exeunt.

RSC, 1993

RSC, 1982

In this scene ...

- Prospero promises that Ferdinand can marry his daughter, Miranda, and commands his spirits to perform an entertainment for them.
- Prospero suddenly remembers that Caliban, Stephano, and Trinculo are plotting to kill him, and tells Ariel to hang some flashy clothing in their way.
- Trinculo and Stephano are distracted by the clothing and start trying it on.
- They are chased out by spirits in the form of hunting dogs.

Ferdinand has passed Prospero's test, and the magician gives him his daughter.

Think about

- Prospero tells Ferdinand that he has given him 'a third of mine own life' (line 3). He presumably means Miranda; but people have puzzled over why he calls her a third. What do you think he might mean?

- How do you react to the way Prospero warns Ferdinand against having sex with Miranda before marriage (lines 14 to 22)? Look in particular at the language he uses.

1 **austerely**: severely
2 **Your compensation**: i.e. Miranda

5 **tender**: offer
   vexations: troubles
7 **strangely**: remarkably well
8 **ratify**: confirm
9 **boast her off**: praise her so highly

11 **halt**: limp

12 **Against an oracle**: even if it were denied by one of the sacred shrines where the gods predict the future

14 **purchased**: bought / worked for
15 **break her virgin-knot**: take her virginity
16 **sanctimonious**: holy
17 **ministered**: carried out
18 **aspersion**: sprinkling of holy water
20 **Sour-eyed disdain**: scorn
   bestrew: scatter
21 **loathly**: disgusting

23 **As Hymen's ... you**: as you hope to be blessed by the god of marriage

24 **fair issue**: beautiful children

26–7 **strong'st ... can**: greatest temptation our evil angel is capable of
29 **edge**: particular joy
30 **or Phoebus' ... below**: i.e. Ferdinand is longing for his wedding night to come more quickly

In front of Prospero's cave.

Enter PROSPERO, FERDINAND, *and* MIRANDA.

PROSPERO   (*To* FERDINAND) If I have too austerely punished you,
Your compensation makes amends: for I
Have given you here a third of mine own life,
Or that for which I live – who once again
I tender to thy hand. All thy vexations   5
Were but my trials of thy love, and thou
Hast strangely stood the test. Here, afore Heaven,
I ratify this my rich gift. O Ferdinand!
Do not smile at me that I boast her off,
For thou shalt find she will outstrip all praise,   10
And make it halt behind her.

FERDINAND   I do believe it,
Against an oracle.

PROSPERO   Then, as my gift, and thine own acquisition
Worthily purchased, take my daughter. But
If thou dost break her virgin-knot before   15
All sanctimonious ceremonies may
With full and holy rite be ministered,
No sweet aspersion shall the heavens let fall
To make this contract grow. But barren hate,
Sour-eyed disdain and discord shall bestrew   20
The union of your bed with weeds so loathly
That you shall hate it both. Therefore take heed,
As Hymen's lamps shall light you!

FERDINAND   As I hope
For quiet days, fair issue, and long life,
With such love as 'tis now, the murkiest den,   25
The most opportune place, the strong'st suggestion
Our worser genius can, shall never melt
Mine honour into lust, to take away
The edge of that day's celebration –
When I shall think, or Phoebus' steeds are foundered,   30
Or Night kept chained below.

Prospero commands Ariel to summon spirits to perform an entertainment for Ferdinand and Miranda.

34 **potent**: powerful

35 **meaner fellows**: inferior fellow spirits

37 **rabble**: gang (of inferior spirits)

39 **Incite**: Encourage

41 **vanity … Art**: amusement

42 **Presently**: At once

43 **with a twink**: in the twinkling of an eye

47 **with … mow**: making faces

---Think about---

• What effect does rhyme have in Ariel's speech (lines 44 to 48)?

• Why do you think Ariel suddenly asks 'Do you love me, master? No?' (line 48)? What might it and Prospero's response (line 49) reveal about the spirit and about Prospero and the relationship between the two?

50 **conceive**: understand

51–2 **give dalliance … rein**: play around sexually
53 **To**: when faced with
Be more abstemious: i.e. hold back from physical / sexual contact
54 **warrant**: promise
55 **The white … heart**: i.e. my sexual purity
56 **Abates … liver**: cools the heat of my passion

PROSPERO	Fairly spoke.
	Sit, then, and talk with her. She is thine own.
	(*He turns away and calls*) What, Ariel! My industrious
	servant, Ariel!

Enter ARIEL.

ARIEL	What would my potent master? Here I am.	
PROSPERO	Thou and thy meaner fellows your last service	35
	Did worthily perform; and I must use you	
	In such another trick. Go bring the rabble –	
	O'er whom I give thee power – here to this place.	
	Incite them to quick motion; for I must	
	Bestow upon the eyes of this young couple	40
	Some vanity of mine Art. It is my promise,	
	And they expect it from me.	
ARIEL	Presently?	
PROSPERO	Ay, with a twink.	
ARIEL	Before you can say, 'Come' and 'Go',	
	And breathe twice, and cry, 'So, so',	45
	Each one, tripping on his toe,	
	Will be here with mop and mow.	
	Do you love me, master? No?	
PROSPERO	Dearly, my delicate Ariel! Do not approach	
	Till thou dost hear me call.	
ARIEL	Well, I conceive.	50

Exit.

PROSPERO	(*To* FERDINAND) Look thou be true! Do not give dalliance	
	Too much the rein. The strongest oaths are straw	
	To the fire i'the blood. Be more abstemious –	
	Or else, good night your vow!	
FERDINAND	I warrant you, sir:	
	The white cold virgin snow upon my heart	55
	Abates the ardour of my liver.	

Spirits appear in the shape of the goddesses Iris and Ceres to celebrate the coming marriage of Ferdinand and Miranda.

57 a corollary: too many
58 want: lack
    pertly: briskly
59 No tongue!: Say nothing!

60 leas: farmland
61 vetches: an animal food

63 meads: meadows
    stover … keep: hay, to feed / protect them
64 banks … brims: river banks, with interwoven willows
65 spongy: moist
    at … hest: decorates at your command
66 cold: pure
    broom-groves: patches of yellow-flowering bushes
67 dismissèd bachelor: rejected lover
68 lass-lorn: suffering the loss of his girl
    poll-clipped: pruned / clipped
69 sea-marge: edge of the sea
70 dost air: take the air
    Queen … sky: i.e. Juno, queen of the gods
71 watery arch: i.e. rainbow
74 amain: swiftly (Juno's chariot was drawn by peacocks)
75 entertain: welcome
78 saffron: yellow
79 Diffusest honey-drops: shed sweet drops of rain
81 bosky: covered in bushes
    unshrubbed down: bare hill country
85 estate: hand over as a gift

> ┌─ **Think about** ─────────
> • The appearance of spirits as Iris, Ceres, and Juno begins the spectacular entertainment (known as a 'masque') that Prospero has promised Miranda and Ferdinand. How would you stage the masque if you were directing the play? Think about how you might show the rainbow and harvest symbols.

PROSPERO	(*To* FERDINAND) Well.
	(*Calling* ARIEL) Now come, my Ariel! Bring a corollary,
	Rather than want a spirit. Appear, and pertly!
	(*To* FERDINAND *and* MIRANDA) No tongue! All eyes! Be
	silent.

Soft music plays. Prospero's entertainment for Ferdinand and Miranda, performed by Spirits, begins.

Enter IRIS *(goddess of the rainbow, Juno's messenger).*

IRIS	Ceres – most bounteous lady! Thy rich leas	60
	Of wheat, rye, barley, vetches, oats, and pease;	
	Thy turfy mountains, where live nibbling sheep,	
	And flat meads thatched with stover, them to keep;	
	Thy banks with pionèd and twillèd brims,	
	Which spongy April at thy hest betrims,	65
	To make cold nymphs chaste crowns; and thy broom-	
	groves,	
	Whose shadow the dismissèd bachelor loves,	
	Being lass-lorn; thy poll-clipped vineyard;	
	And thy sea-marge, sterile and rocky-hard,	
	Where thou thyself dost air – the Queen o'the sky,	70
	Whose watery arch and messenger am I,	
	Bids thee leave these – and with her sovereign grace,	
	Here, on this grass-plot, in this very place,	
	To come and sport. Her peacocks fly amain!	
	Approach, rich Ceres, her to entertain.	75

Enter CERES *(goddess of harvest).*

CERES	Hail, many-coloured messenger, that ne'er	
	Dost disobey the wife of Jupiter –	
	Who, with thy saffron wings, upon my flowers	
	Diffusest honey-drops, refreshing showers;	
	And with each end of thy blue bow dost crown	80
	My bosky acres and my unshrubbed down,	
	Rich scarf to my proud earth. Why hath thy Queen	
	Summoned me hither, to this short-grassed green?	
IRIS	A contract of true love to celebrate –	
	And some donation freely to estate	85
	On the blest lovers.	

Another spirit appears as Juno, queen of the gods. Juno and Ceres bless the coming marriage of Ferdinand and Miranda.

87 **Venus**: the goddess of love and sex
 her son: Cupid

89 **dusky Dis**: dark Pluto (who abducted Ceres' daughter down to the underworld)

90 **blind**: Cupid is usually shown blindfolded
 scandalled: shameful

91 **forsworn**: promised to avoid

92 **deity**: divine self

93 **Paphos**: Venus's sacred place in Cyprus

94–5 **done … charm**: cast some spell to make them have sex

96 **no … paid**: they will not have sex

97 **Till … lighted**: until they are married

98 **Mars's hot minion**: the lustful lover of Mars (i.e. Venus)

99 **waspish-headed**: bad-tempered

101 **be … out**: only behave like any other boy

102 **her gait**: the way she moves

104 **twain**: pair

105 **issue**: children

107 **increasing**: having children

108 **still**: always

110 **foison plenty**: plentiful harvest

111 **garners**: granaries

113 **burden**: crop

114–5 **Spring … harvest**: i.e. with no winter in between

Think about

- The spirits are acting at Prospero's command. Why is it important that Venus, goddess of love and sex, and her son Cupid, should not be part of these celebrations? Look at lines 86 to 101.

CERES   Tell me, heavenly bow,
                 If Venus or her son, as thou dost know,
                 Do now attend the Queen? Since they did plot
                 The means that dusky Dis my daughter got,
                 Her and her blind boy's scandalled company   90
                 I have forsworn.

IRIS   Of her society
                 Be not afraid. I met her deity
                 Cutting the clouds towards Paphos, and her son
                 Dove-drawn with her. Here thought they to have done
                 Some wanton charm upon this man and maid,   95
                 Whose vows are, that no bed-right shall be paid
                 Till Hymen's torch be lighted. But in vain –
                 Mars's hot minion is returned again.
                 Her waspish-headed son has broke his arrows,
                 Swears he will shoot no more, but play with sparrows,   100
                 And be a boy right out.

JUNO *(Queen of the gods), who has descended from above the scene, alights and enters.*

CERES   Highest Queen of state,
                 Great Juno, comes – I know her by her gait.

JUNO   How does my bounteous sister? Go with me
                 To bless this twain, that they may prosperous be,
                 And honoured in their issue!   105

They sing.

JUNO   Honour, riches, marriage-blessing,
                 Long continuance, and increasing,
                 Hourly joys be still upon you!
                 Juno sings her blessing on you.

CERES   Earth's increase, foison plenty,   110
                 Barns and garners never empty;
                 Vines with clustering bunches growing;
                 Plants with goodly burden bowing;
                 Spring come to you at the farthest
                 In the very end of harvest!   115
                 Scarcity and want shall shun you;
                 Ceres' blessing so is on you.

In the middle of the entertainment, Prospero suddenly remembers that Caliban, Trinculo, and Stephano are plotting against him.

119   Harmonious charmingly: enchantingly musical
May I be bold: Would I be right

121   their confines: the places where they are allowed to live

122   fancies: ideas

123   wondered: 1 to be wondered at; 2 able to perform wonders

124   Paradise: the garden of Eden

127   marred: spoiled

128   Naiads: water-nymphs

129   sedged: woven from rushes

130   crisp channels: rippling streams

132   temperate: sexually pure

134   sickle-men: harvesters / reapers

137   encounter: join
138   footing: dance

140   confederates: allies / fellow-plotters

142   Avoid: Be gone

Think about

• Shakespeare seems to have invented the word 'windring' in line 128. What do you think it means?

• Prospero has been totally in command so far. So how do you think he comes to forget Caliban's plot to kill him (lines 139 to 141)?

FERDINAND	This is a most majestic vision, and Harmonious charmingly. May I be bold To think these spirits?
PROSPERO	Spirits, which by mine Art **120** I have from their confines called to enact My present fancies.
FERDINAND	Let me live here ever! So rare a wondered father and a wife Makes this place Paradise.

JUNO *and* CERES *whisper together, and give another task to* IRIS.

PROSPERO	(*To* FERDINAND *and* MIRANDA) Sweet, now, silence! Juno and Ceres whisper seriously. **125** There's something else to do. Hush, and be mute, Or else our spell is marred.
IRIS	You nymphs, called Naiads, of the windring brooks, With your sedged crowns and ever-harmless looks, Leave your crisp channels, and on this green land **130** Answer your summons. Juno does command! Come, temperate nymphs, and help to celebrate A contract of true love. Be not too late.

Enter Nymphs.

You sunburned sickle-men, of August weary,
Come hither from the furrow, and be merry.   **135**
Make holiday! Your rye-straw hats put on,
And these fresh nymphs encounter every one
In country footing.

Enter REAPERS. *They join with the* NYMPHS *in a graceful dance, towards the end of which* PROSPERO *starts suddenly, and speaks. There is a strange, hollow, and confused noise – and the* NYMPHS *and* REAPERS *vanish sorrowfully away.*

PROSPERO	(*Aside*) I had forgot that foul conspiracy Of the beast Caliban and his confederates **140** Against my life! The minute of their plot Is almost come. (*To the Spirits*) Well done! Avoid. No more!

Prospero explains the disappearance of the masque to Ferdinand and admits that he is greatly disturbed. He tells Ariel that they must prepare for the encounter with Caliban.

Think about

- Prospero says that the whole world, 'the great globe itself', will one day 'dissolve' (lines 153 to 154). What else can the phrase 'the great globe' refer to? What is the effect of this double meaning?

- Prospero claims that 'We are such stuff As dreams are made on; and our little life Is rounded with a sleep' (lines 156 to 158). What does this suggest about his view of life and death?

- In lines 158 to 160, Prospero talks about his 'weakness' and being 'vexed'. What do you think has caused him to feel like this?

144 **works**: disturbs

145 **so distempered**: in such a troubled mood
146 **movèd sort**: troubled state

148 **revels**: entertainments

151 **baseless ... vision**: i.e. the spectacle has no foundation in reality

154 **all ... inherit**: all the people who will live in it or possess it
155 **insubstantial pageant**: show without any physical reality
156 **rack**: wisp of cloud
158 **rounded**: 1 ended; 2 surrounded
vexed: troubled
160 **with my infirmity**: by my weakness
162 **A turn ... walk**: I will walk up and down for a while
163 **beating**: disturbed

164 **with a thought**: as soon as I think of you

165 **cleave to**: follow exactly

167 **presented**: 1 acted the part of; 2 produced the masque of; 3 introduced

170 **varlets**: villains

FERDINAND	This is strange. Your father's in some passion
	That works him strongly.
MIRANDA	Never till this day
	Saw I him touched with anger, so distempered. 145
PROSPERO	You do look, my son, in a movèd sort,
	As if you were dismayed. Be cheerful, sir.
	Our revels now are ended. These our actors,
	As I foretold you, were all spirits – and
	Are melted into air, into thin air. 150
	And, like the baseless fabric of this vision,
	The cloud-capped towers, the gorgeous palaces,
	The solemn temples, the great globe itself,
	Yea, all which it inherit, shall dissolve,
	And, like this insubstantial pageant faded, 155
	Leave not a rack behind. We are such stuff
	As dreams are made on; and our little life
	Is rounded with a sleep. Sir, I am vexed.
	Bear with my weakness: my old brain is troubled.
	Be not disturbed with my infirmity. 160
	If you be pleased, retire into my cell,
	And there repose. A turn or two I'll walk,
	To still my beating mind.
FERDINAND	
AND MIRANDA	We wish your peace.

Exit MIRANDA, *with* FERDINAND.

PROSPERO	(*Calling* ARIEL) Come with a thought! (*To* FERDINAND
	and MIRANDA) I thank thee. Ariel, come!

Enter ARIEL.

ARIEL	Thy thoughts I cleave to. What's thy pleasure?
PROSPERO	Spirit, 165
	We must prepare to meet with Caliban.
ARIEL	Ay, my commander. When I presented Ceres,
	I thought to have told thee of it – but I feared
	Lest I might anger thee.
PROSPERO	Say again, where didst thou leave these varlets? 170

Prospero hears that Ariel has led Caliban, Trinculo, and Stephano through bushes and into a stinking, muddy pond. Prospero and Ariel then prepare another trap for them.

171 **red-hot**: fired up
172 **smote**: struck

174–5 **bending ... project**: pursuing their plan (to kill Prospero)
175 **tabor**: drum
176 **unbacked colts**: untamed horses
177 **Advanced**: raised
178 **As**: as though
179 **lowing**: mooing

182 **filthy-mantled**: covered in foul scum

184 **O'erstunk**: stank more than

186 **trumpery**: trashy clothing
187 **stale**: bait

189 **Nurture**: careful upbringing
190 **Humanely**: i.e. like a kind human being
192 **cankers**: turns bad
193 **Even to roaring**: to the point where they cry out

193 **line**: 1 clothes line; 2 lime tree

Think about

- Shakespeare often chooses to have events reported rather than shown on stage. How could Ariel's speech (lines 171 to 184) be shown in a film version? How would you choose to present it if you were directing a film?

197 **played ... us**: made fools of us

ARIEL	I told you, sir, they were red-hot with drinking –
	So full of valour that they smote the air
	For breathing in their faces; beat the ground
	For kissing of their feet – yet always bending
	Towards their project. Then I beat my tabor: 175
	At which, like unbacked colts, they pricked their ears,
	Advanced their eyelids, lifted up their noses
	As they smelt music. So I charmed their ears,
	That, calf-like, they my lowing followed, through
	Toothed briers, sharp furzes, pricking gorse, and thorns, 180
	Which entered their frail shins. At last I left them
	I'the filthy-mantled pool beyond your cell,
	There dancing up to the chins, that the foul lake
	O'erstunk their feet.

PROSPERO This was well done, my bird!
Thy shape invisible retain thou still. **185**
The trumpery in my house, go bring it hither,
For stale to catch these thieves.

ARIEL I go, I go.

Exit.

PROSPERO A devil, a born devil, on whose nature
Nurture can never stick – on whom my pains,
Humanely taken, all, all lost, quite lost! **190**
And as with age his body uglier grows,
So his mind cankers. I will plague them all,
Even to roaring.

Re-enter ARIEL, *with a load of flashy, shining clothing.*

Come, hang them on this line.

Enter CALIBAN, STEPHANO, *and* TRINCULO, *soaked and dirty.*
(ARIEL *and* PROSPERO *are invisible to them.*)

CALIBAN Pray you, tread softly, that the blind mole may not
Hear a foot fall. We now are near his cell. **195**

STEPHANO Monster, your fairy, which you say is a harmless fairy,
has done little better than played the Jack with us.

As Trinculo and Stephano approach Prospero's cell, they are distracted by some cheap but flashy clothing hung out there by Ariel.

199 in great indignation: extremely irritated

205 hoodwink this mischance: make you forget this misfortune

210 more: more important

212 fetch off: recover

212–13 be ... labour: will get completely immersed in the pool by trying to retrieve it

218 aye: ever

220 peer: nobleman

223 We ... frippery: This isn't stuff you find in a second-hand clothes shop

---

Think about

• An 'oxymoron' is a phrase which seems to contradict itself. What do you think Caliban means by 'good mischief' (line 216)?

• What might the 'wardrobe' of clothes look like on stage (line 221)?

• Caliban describes the wardrobe as 'but trash' (line 222). Why are Stephano and Trinculo attracted – and distracted – by it? What does it reveal about them?

TRINCULO	Monster, I do smell all horse-piss – at which my nose is in great indignation.
STEPHANO	So is mine. Do you hear, monster? If I should take a **200** displeasure against you, look you –
TRINCULO	Thou wert but a lost monster.
CALIBAN	Good my lord, give me thy favour still.
	Be patient, for the prize I'll bring thee to
	Shall hoodwink this mischance. Therefore speak softly. **205**
	All's hushed as midnight yet.
TRINCULO	Ay, but to lose our bottles in the pool!
STEPHANO	There is not only disgrace and dishonour in that, monster, but an infinite loss.
TRINCULO	That's more to me than my wetting. Yet this is your **210** harmless fairy, monster.
STEPHANO	I will fetch off my bottle, though I be o'er ears for my labour.
CALIBAN	Prithee, my King, be quiet. See'st thou here:
	This is the mouth o'the cell. No noise, and enter. **215**
	Do that good mischief which may make this island
	Thine own for ever, and I, thy Caliban,
	For aye thy foot-licker.
STEPHANO	Give me thy hand. I do begin to have bloody thoughts.
TRINCULO	O King Stephano! O peer! O worthy Stephano! **220**
	Look what wardrobe here is for thee!
CALIBAN	Let it alone, thou fool! It is but trash.
TRINCULO	O, ho, monster! We know what belongs to a frippery.
	O King Stephano!

They take and try on the clothes that ARIEL *has left.*

STEPHANO	Put off that gown, Trinculo. By this hand, I'll have that **225** gown!
TRINCULO	Thy grace shall have it.

Stephano and Trinculo ignore Caliban's warning to leave the clothes alone. All three are suddenly chased by spirits, controlled by Prospero and Ariel, in the form of hunting dogs.

- Stephano's comments about the jerkin being 'under the line' and 'bald' (lines 234 to 235) are very obscure references for a modern audience. How can humour like that be successfully conveyed on stage? Does it matter if it is not understood?

- How do you think 'Spirits in the form of large hunting-dogs' might have been represented on Shakespeare's stage? If you were a director, how would you choose to show them in a production today?

228 **dropsy**: a disease
    drown: suffocate
229 **luggage**: rubbish you have to lug about

234 **jerkin**: jacket
234–5 **under the line ... bald**: possibly a reference to voyagers who had their head shaved when crossing the equator
236 **Do, do**: Excellent
    by ... level: with builders' tools, i.e. skilfully
239 **pass of pate**: stroke of wit
241 **lime**: a sticky substance that clothing would adhere to

244 **barnacles**: types of shellfish or geese

246 **lay-to your fingers**: put your fingers to work
247 **hogshead**: barrel
248 **Go to**: Get moving

251–3 **Mountain ... hark!**: Prospero and Ariel (who are invisible) imitate the shouts of hunters encouraging their hounds

CALIBAN	The dropsy drown this fool! What do you mean To dote thus on such luggage? Let't alone, And do the murder first! If he awake, 230 From toe to crown he'll fill our skins with pinches, Make *us* strange stuff.
STEPHANO	Be you quiet, monster. Mistress line, is not this my jerkin? Now is the jerkin under the line: now, jerkin, you are like to lose your hair, and prove a bald jerkin. 235
TRINCULO	Do, do! We steal by line and level, an it like your grace.
STEPHANO	I thank thee for that jest: here's a garment for it. Wit shall not go unrewarded while I am king of this country. 'Steal by line and level' is an excellent pass of pate! There's another garment for it. 240
TRINCULO	Monster, come, put some lime upon your fingers, and away with the rest.
CALIBAN	I will have none on't! We shall lose our time, And all be turned to barnacles, or to apes With foreheads villainous low. 245
STEPHANO	Monster, lay-to your fingers! Help to bear this away where my hogshead of wine is, or I'll turn you out of my kingdom. Go to, carry this!
TRINCULO	And this!
STEPHANO	Ay, and this. 250

A sudden noise of hunting-horns and dogs. Enter SPIRITS, *in the form of large hunting-dogs. They chase* STEPHANO, TRINCULO, *and* CALIBAN *to and fro, with* ARIEL *and* PROSPERO *shouting to urge them on.*

PROSPERO	Hey, Mountain, hey!
ARIEL	Silver! There it goes, Silver!
PROSPERO	Fury, Fury! There! Tyrant, there! Hark, hark!

CALIBAN, STEPHANO, *and* TRINCULO *are chased away.*

Prospero now has all his
enemies where he wants them.

254 **charge**: order
     grind: torment
255 **dry convulsions**: cramps
256 **aged cramps**: pains that old people
     suffer
     pinch-spotted: bruised by pinches
257 **pard**: leopard
     cat-o'-mountain: wildcat

261 **little**: little while

Think about

• In lines 254 to 257,
  Prospero again orders Ariel
  to use physical torment to
  punish people who have
  offended him. What other
  kinds of punishment does
  Prospero use?

• How do all these
  punishments affect your
  view of Prospero?

	Go charge my goblins that they grind their joints	
	With dry convulsions; shorten up their sinews	255
	With aged cramps – and more pinch-spotted make them	
	Than pard or cat-o'-mountain!	

ARIEL   Hark, they roar!

PROSPERO   Let them be hunted soundly. At this hour
Lies at my mercy all mine enemies.
Shortly shall all my labours end, and thou   260
Shalt have the air at freedom. For a little
Follow, and do me service.

Exeunt.

155

RSC, 1982

RSC, 1998

RSC, 1993

RSC, 1993

RSC, 2002

RSC, 1970

RSC, 1993

In this scene ...

- Prospero vows to give up his magic art. When his enemies enter under a spell, he addresses them in turn.
- Alonso asks Prospero to forgive him. When he grieves over the loss of his son, Prospero reveals Ferdinand and Miranda.
- Prospero invites Alonso and his companions to spend the night at his cave before sailing home to Naples the next day.
- Finally, Prospero releases Ariel, and ends the play.

Ariel tells Prospero where all his enemies are. Ariel says that Prospero would sympathise with them in their suffering if he saw them. Prospero agrees that he will not take further revenge against them.

1   **gather to a head**: near its climax
2   **crack**: fail
2–3 **time ... carriage**: i.e. there is not much time to go
4   **On**: Approaching

7   **How fares ... ?**: How are ... getting on?

8   **gave in charge**: instructed me

10 **weather-fends**: protects from the wind
11 **till your release**: till you release them
12 **distracted**: out of their wits

17 **eaves of reeds**: thatched roofs
    charm: magic spell
18 **affections**: feelings

Think about

- Prospero clearly now has everybody where he wants them. Predict what he will do to each person.
- How important to Prospero is Ariel's comment about feeling sympathy for the King and his party (lines 17 to 20)?

23 **relish all as**: experience just as

25 **struck to the quick**: deeply wounded
27 **take part**: take sides
27–8 **The rarer ... vengeance**: It is better to forgive than to take revenge

In front of Prospero's cave.

Enter PROSPERO *in his magic cloak, and* ARIEL.

PROSPERO   Now does my project gather to a head.
            My charms crack not, my spirits obey; and time
            Goes upright with his carriage. How's the day?

ARIEL   On the sixth hour – at which time, my lord,
            You said our work should cease.

PROSPERO   I did say so,   5
            When first I raised the tempest. Say, my spirit,
            How fares the King and's followers?

ARIEL   Confined together
            In the same fashion as you gave in charge,
            Just as you left them: all prisoners, sir,
            In the lime-grove which weather-fends your cell.   10
            They cannot budge till your release. The King,
            His brother, and yours, abide all three distracted,
            And the remainder mourning over them,
            Brimful of sorrow and dismay – but chiefly
            Him you termed, sir, 'The good old lord, Gonzalo'.   15
            His tears run down his beard, like winter's drops
            From eaves of reeds. Your charm so strongly works 'em,
            That if you now beheld them, your affections
            Would become tender.

PROSPERO   Dost thou think so, spirit?

ARIEL   Mine would, sir, were I human.

PROSPERO   And mine shall.   20
            Hast thou, which art but air, a touch, a feeling
            Of their afflictions, and shall not myself –
            One of their kind, that relish all as sharply
            Passion as they – be kindlier moved than thou art?
            Though with their high wrongs I am struck to the quick, 25
            Yet with my nobler reason 'gainst my fury
            Do I take part. The rarer action is
            In virtue than in vengeance. They being penitent,

Prospero says that he will give up his magic. Alonso and his companions enter, under a spell.

29 **sole drift**: single aim

29–30 **doth ... further**: i.e. he will take no further action against them

35 **Neptune**: i.e. the sea
36 **demi-puppets**: fairies
37 **green sour ringlets**: 'fairy rings' in the grass
38 **Whereof ... bites**: which the sheep will not eat
40 **curfew**: evening warning bell

43 **azured vault**: blue sky

45 **rifted**: split in two
    Jove: Jupiter, king of the gods
46 **bolt**: thunderbolt (Jupiter's weapon)
    promontory: headland
47 **spurs**: roots
50 **rough**: 1 crude; 2 violent in its effects
51 **abjure**: give up
53 **work mine end**: complete my intended effect
54 **airy charm**: music, sounding in the air, which works a magic spell
56–7 **And deeper ... book**: I will drown my book at a greater depth than has ever been measured

---

Think about

- What is Prospero giving up? Why is he giving it up? Look at lines 33 to 57.

- Many people have seen Prospero's speech as Shakespeare's farewell to the stage, since it was written around the time of his retirement. What is there about Prospero and his 'art' which makes him a parallel for Shakespeare? Why might this speech be seen as Shakespeare's personal statement that he is giving up writing?

	The sole drift of my purpose doth extend	
	Not a frown further. Go release them, Ariel.	30

The sole drift of my purpose doth extend
Not a frown further. Go release them, Ariel.   30
My charms I'll break, their senses I'll restore,
And they shall be themselves.

ARIEL   I'll fetch them, sir.

Exit.

PROSPERO   Ye elves of hills, brooks, standing lakes, and groves;
And ye that on the sands with printless foot
Do chase the ebbing Neptune, and do fly him   35
When he comes back; you demi-puppets that
By moonshine do the green sour ringlets make,
Whereof the ewe not bites; and you whose pastime
Is to make midnight mushrooms, that rejoice
To hear the solemn curfew – by whose aid   40
(Weak masters though ye be) I have bedimmed
The noontide sun, called forth the mutinous winds,
And 'twixt the green sea and the azured vault
Set roaring war. To the dread rattling thunder
Have I given fire, and rifted Jove's stout oak   45
With his own bolt. The strong-based promontory
Have I made shake, and by the spurs plucked up
The pine and cedar. Graves at my command
Have waked their sleepers, oped, and let 'em forth
By my so potent Art. But this rough magic   50
I here abjure. And, when I have required
Some heavenly music (which even now I do),
To work mine end upon their senses that
This airy charm is for, I'll break my staff,
Bury it certain fathoms in the earth,   55
And deeper than did ever plummet sound
I'll drown my book.

Solemn music plays.

PROSPERO *marks a magic circle on the ground.*

Re-enter ARIEL. *King* ALONSO *follows, moving as if driven mad, with* GONZALO *tending to him.* SEBASTIAN *and* ANTONIO *follow, also appearing maddened, accompanied by* ADRIAN *and* FRANCISCO. *All enter Prospero's magic circle and stand there, still, under the power of his spell.* PROSPERO *watches them, then speaks.*

Prospero addresses the men caught in his magic circle. Alonso, Sebastian, and Antonio begin to come out of their trances as the spell begins to fade. None of them yet realise who Prospero is.

59 **fancy**: imagination

63 **sociable**: sympathetic
64 **apace**: quickly

67–8 **chase … reason**: dispel the fogginess in their minds that makes them incapable of understanding
70–1 **pay … Home**: fully reward your kind actions

73 **furtherer**: supporter
74 **pinched**: tormented

76 **Expelled**: i.e. refused to feel
    nature: natural brotherly feelings

81 **reasonable shore**: i.e. their minds

84 **rapier**: sword

85 **discase me**: remove my magic robe
86 **As I … Milan**: dressed as I used to be when I was Duke of Milan
87 **ere**: before

90 **couch**: sit / rest

---Think about

• If you were directing this scene, where would you have the characters stand in relation to one another? Think about the order in which Prospero addresses them and the ways in which they might respond. (Look carefully at the stage direction at line 57.)

A solemn air, and the best comforter
To an unsettled fancy, cure thy brains,
Now useless, boiled within thy skull! There stand,   **60**
For you are spell-stopped.
Holy Gonzalo, honourable man,
Mine eyes, ev'n sociable to the show of thine,
Fall fellowly drops. The charm dissolves apace –
And as the morning steals upon the night,   **65**
Melting the darkness, so their rising senses
Begin to chase the ignorant fumes that mantle
Their clearer reason. O good Gonzalo,
My true preserver, and a loyal sir
To him thou follow'st! I will pay thy graces   **70**
Home both in word and deed. Most cruelly
Didst thou, Alonso, use me and my daughter.
Thy brother was a furtherer in the act.
Thou art pinched for't now, Sebastian! Flesh and blood,
You, brother mine, that entertained ambition,   **75**
Expelled remorse and nature – whom, with Sebastian,
Whose inward pinches therefore are most strong,
Would here have killed your King – I do forgive thee,
Unnatural though thou art! Their understanding
Begins to swell – and the approaching tide   **80**
Will shortly fill the reasonable shore,
That now lies foul and muddy. Not one of them
That yet looks on me, or would know me. Ariel,
Fetch me the hat and rapier in my cell.

Exit ARIEL.

I will discase me, and myself present   **85**
As I was sometime Milan. Quickly, Spirit!
Thou shalt ere long be free.

Re-enter ARIEL, *with hat and rapier. As he helps to dress*
PROSPERO, *and remove his magic cloak, he sings.*

ARIEL   Where the bee sucks, there suck I.
In a cowslip's bell I lie.
There I couch when owls do cry.   **90**
On the bat's back I do fly –
After summer merrily.
  Merrily, merrily shall I live now
Under the blossom that hangs on the bough!

Prospero tells Ariel to fetch the Master and Boatswain from the ship. Alonso and his companions are released from the spell and Prospero greets them. Alonso recognises Prospero and asks for forgiveness.

96 So, so, so: That's right (to Ariel as he finishes dressing him)

101 presently: at once

108 For more assurance: i.e. to give you further proof

111 thou be'st: you are
112 enchanted ... abuse: magic trick to deceive
113 late: recently
115 amends: is getting better
116–17 This must ... story: This – if it is really happening – calls for an extraordinary explanation

---

Think about

• How does Alonso react when he recognises Prospero (lines 111 to 120)?

• What does Alonso's reaction tell us about him?

PROSPERO	Why, that's my dainty Ariel! I shall miss thee – 95
	But yet thou shalt have freedom. So, so, so.
	To the King's ship, invisible as thou art.
	There shalt thou find the mariners asleep
	Under the hatches. The master and the boatswain
	Being awake, enforce them to this place, 100
	And presently, I prithee.
ARIEL	I drink the air before me, and return
	Or ere your pulse twice beat.

Exit.

GONZALO	All torment, trouble, wonder and amazement
	Inhabits here. Some heavenly power guide us 105
	Out of this fearful country!
PROSPERO	Behold, sir King,
	The wrongèd Duke of Milan, Prospero.
	For more assurance that a living prince
	Does now speak to thee, I embrace thy body –
	(***Embraces*** ALONSO)
	And to thee and thy company I bid 110
	A hearty welcome.
ALONSO	Whether thou be'st he or no,
	Or some enchanted trifle to abuse me,
	As late I have been, I not know. Thy pulse
	Beats, as of flesh and blood – and, since I saw thee,
	Th'affliction of my mind amends, with which, 115
	I fear, a madness held me. This must crave –
	An if this be at all – a most strange story.
	Thy dukedom I resign, and do entreat
	Thou pardon me my wrongs. But how should Prospero
	Be living and be here?
PROSPERO	(*To* GONZALO) First, noble friend, 120
	Let me embrace thine age, whose honour cannot
	Be measured or confined. (***Embraces him***)
GONZALO	Whether this be
	Or be not, I'll not swear!

Prospero says that he forgives his brother, Antonio. Alonso mourns the loss of his son, Ferdinand, and Prospero tells him that he himself has recently lost a daughter.

123–4 do yet … isle: are still affected by the island's illusions

126 brace: pair
127 pluck … you: cause the King to be angry with you
128 justify: prove

132 rankest: most disgusting
133 perforce: necessarily

135 particulars … preservation: details of how you were saved

139 woe: sorry

142 of … grace: by whose tender mercy
143 sovereign: supreme

145 as late: as it is recent

Think about

- Many people have argued that Prospero never does forgive his brother, despite what he says in lines 130 to 134. Does he forgive him or not, in your opinion? Why doesn't Antonio reply?

- How does Prospero react when Alonso recalls the loss of Ferdinand (lines 134 to 141)? Why do you think he responds to Alonso in this way?

PROSPERO	You do yet taste

Some subtleties o'the isle, that will not let you
Believe things certain. Welcome, my friends all! 125
(*Aside to* SEBASTIAN *and* ANTONIO) But you, my brace of
    lords, were I so minded,
I here could pluck his highness' frown upon you,
And justify you traitors. At this time
I will tell no tales.

SEBASTIAN   (*Aside*) The devil speaks in him!

PROSPERO   No.
(*To* ANTONIO) For you, most wicked sir, whom to call
    brother 130
Would even infect my mouth, I do forgive
Thy rankest fault – all of them – and require
My dukedom of thee: which perforce, I know,
Thou must restore.

ALONSO   If thou be'st Prospero,
Give us particulars of thy preservation, 135
How thou hast met us here, who three hours since
Were wrecked upon this shore: where I have lost –
How sharp the point of this remembrance is! –
My dear son Ferdinand.

PROSPERO   I am woe for't, sir.

ALONSO Irreparable is the loss: and patience 140
Says it is past her cure.

PROSPERO   I rather think
You have not sought her help, of whose soft grace
For the like loss I have her sovereign aid,
And rest myself content.

ALONSO   You the like loss!

PROSPERO As great to me, as late – and, supportable 145
To make the dear loss, have I means much weaker
Than you may call to comfort you – for I
Have lost my daughter.

ALONSO   A daughter?
O heavens, that they were living both in Naples,

Prospero reveals Ferdinand and
Miranda playing chess.

150 **That they were**: If only they could be
151 **mudded ... bed**: buried in the mud of
the sea-bed

154 **do ... admire**: are so amazed
155–6 **devour ... truth**: cannot trust their
reason or their eyes

159 **very**: same
160 **of**: from

163 **a chronicle ... day**: a story that needs
days to tell
164 **relation**: report

167 **abroad**: i.e. anywhere else

169 **requite**: repay

Think about

• Parents often talk about
'losing' a child when he or
she gets married. But how
far do you feel that
Prospero really does believe
that he has 'lost' Miranda
'In this last tempest'? Look
at lines 145 to 153.

172 **play me false**: are cheating me

174 **wrangle**: compete with me (i.e. fairly
or not)

• How might Miranda and
Ferdinand have been
'revealed' on Shakespeare's
stage? How would you
manage it if you were
staging it today?

176 **vision**: illusion
177 **twice lose**: because he thought him
dead and would now lose him again if
this turned out to be merely an illusion

	The King and Queen there! That they were, I wish	**150**
	Myself were mudded in that oozy bed	
	Where my son lies! When did you lose your daughter?	

PROSPERO   In this last tempest. I perceive these lords
And this encounter do so much admire
That they devour their reason, and scarce think   **155**
Their eyes do offices of truth, their words
Are natural breath. But, howsoe'er you have
Been jostled from your senses, know for certain
That I am Prospero, and that very duke
Which was thrust forth of Milan – who most strangely   **160**
Upon this shore where you were wrecked, was landed,
To be the lord on't. No more yet of this –
For 'tis a chronicle of day by day,
Not a relation for a breakfast, nor
Befitting this first meeting. Welcome, sir.   **165**
This cell's my court. Here have I few attendants,
And subjects none abroad. Pray you, look in.
My dukedom since you have given me again,
I will requite you with as good a thing –
At least bring forth a wonder, to content ye   **170**
As much as me my dukedom.

PROSPERO *now reveals* FERDINAND *and* MIRANDA, *playing chess together.*

MIRANDA   Sweet lord, you play me false.

FERDINAND   No, my dearest love,
I would not for the world.

MIRANDA   Yes – for a score of kingdoms you should wrangle,
And I would call it fair play.

ALONSO   If this prove   **175**
A vision of the island, one dear son
Shall I twice lose.

SEBASTIAN   A most high miracle!

FERDINAND   Though the seas threaten, they are merciful!
I have cursed them without cause.

He kneels before his father, ALONSO.

Miranda expresses her wonder at the people she sees before her. Alonso joyfully greets his son, Ferdinand. He asks Miranda to forgive him for once helping to overthrow her father as Duke of Milan.

180 **compass thee about**: surround you

183 **brave**: fine and noble

186 **Your ... be**: You cannot have known each other longer than
187 **severed**: separated

195 **second father**: i.e. father-in-law

---Think about---

- As an actor, in what tone would you deliver Prospero's response "Tis new to thee' (line 184)?

- Bearing in mind the irony in Caliban's use of 'brave' (see page 98), what comment would you make on Miranda's delight in the 'goodly creatures' she now sees and the 'brave new world, That has such people in't' (lines 182 to 184)?

199 **burden our remembrances**: weigh down our memories
200 **heaviness**: grief
inly: inwardly / without showing it

203 **chalked forth**: i.e. marked out

ALONSO   Now all the blessings
            Of a glad father compass thee about!   180
            Arise, and say how thou cam'st here.

MIRANDA   O wonder!
            How many goodly creatures are there here!
            How beauteous mankind is! O brave new world,
            That has such people in't!

PROSPERO   'Tis new to thee.

ALONSO   (*To* FERDINAND) What is this maid with whom thou
                wast at play?   185
            Your eld'st acquaintance cannot be three hours!
            Is she the goddess that hath severed us,
            And brought us thus together?

FERDINAND   Sir, she is mortal:
            But by immortal Providence she's mine.
            I chose her when I could not ask my father   190
            For his advice, nor thought I had one. She
            Is daughter to this famous Duke of Milan,
            Of whom so often I have heard renown,
            But never saw before. Of whom I have
            Received a second life; and second father   195
            This lady makes him to me.

ALONSO   I am hers.
            But O – how oddly will it sound that I
            Must ask my child forgiveness!

PROSPERO   There, sir, stop.
            Let us not burden our remembrances with
            A heaviness that's gone.

GONZALO   I have inly wept,   200
            Or should have spoke ere this. Look down, you gods,
            And on this couple drop a blessèd crown!
            For it is you that have chalked forth the way
            Which brought us hither.

ALONSO   I say 'Amen', Gonzalo!

As Gonzalo is expressing his joy, Ariel brings in the ship's Master and Boatswain. The Boatswain explains how they were released.

205 **Milan ... Milan**: the Duke ... the city
his issue: i.e. Miranda's children

214 **still**: always

218 **blasphemy**: you blasphemous man
219 **That ... o'erboard**: who forces godliness off the ship with your swearing

223 **but ... since**: only three hours ago
gave out: reported
224 **tight and yare**: watertight and shipshape
bravely: finely

226 **tricksy**: clever

227–8 **strengthen ... stranger**: become stranger and stranger

230 **dead of sleep**: fast asleep
231 **clapped ... hatches**: i.e. locked up under the deck
232 **but even now**: only a few moments ago

> **Think about**
>
> - How do the reactions of Antonio and Sebastian differ from those of Gonzalo and Alonso?
>
> - How would you account for the reactions of Antonio and Sebastian?

GONZALO	Was Milan thrust from Milan, that his issue 205

GONZALO Was Milan thrust from Milan, that his issue 205
Should become Kings of Naples? O, rejoice
Beyond a common joy! And set it down
With gold on lasting pillars! In one voyage
Did Claribel her husband find at Tunis,
And Ferdinand, her brother, found a wife 210
Where he himself was lost – Prospero his dukedom
In a poor isle – and all of us ourselves
When no man was his own!

ALONSO (*To* FERDINAND *and* MIRANDA) Give me your hands.
Let grief and sorrow still embrace his heart
That doth not wish you joy!

GONZALO Be it so! Amen! 215

Enter ARIEL, *bringing the ship's* MASTER *and* BOATSWAIN, *amazed
and confused by their experience.*

O look, sir, look, sir! Here is more of us.
I prophesied, if a gallows were on land,
This fellow could not drown. Now, blasphemy,
That swear'st grace o'erboard, not an oath on shore?
Hast thou no mouth by land? What is the news? 220

BOATSWAIN The best news is, that we have safely found
Our King, and company. The next, our ship –
Which, but three glasses since, we gave out split –
Is tight and yare and bravely rigged as when
We first put out to sea.

ARIEL (*Aside to* PROSPERO) Sir, all this service 225
Have I done since I went.

PROSPERO (*Aside to* ARIEL) My tricksy Spirit!

ALONSO These are not natural events: they strengthen
From strange to stranger. Say, how came you hither?

BOATSWAIN If I did think, sir, I were well awake,
I'd strive to tell you. We were dead of sleep, 230
And – how we know not – all clapped under hatches;
Where, but even now, with strange and several noises
Of roaring, shrieking, howling, jingling chains,
And more diversity of sounds, all horrible,

Prospero promises that he will
soon explain everything to
Alonso. Ariel brings in Caliban
with Stephano and Trinculo.

236 **trim**: garments

238 **Cap'ring to eye**: dancing with joy at
the sight of
On a trice: in a split-second
240 **moping**: in a daze

241 **Bravely, my diligence**: brilliantly done,
my hard worker

244 **conduct**: conductor / director
oracle: god's voice (which could be
consulted at a sacred shrine)
245 **rectify our knowledge**: correct our
understanding
246 **infest**: trouble
beating on: worrying about
247 **At picked leisure**: At a convenient time
248 **single**: i.e. he wants to speak to Alonso
alone, or without interruption
249–50 **every ... accidents**: every one of these
occurrences

255 **odd**: unaccounted for / extra

Think about

• What can you tell about
Prospero's attitude to
Alonso from the way he
speaks to him in lines 245
to 255? Has Prospero
forgiven him for having
supported Antonio?

256 **shift for**: look after

257 **Coragio**: Courage

259 **If ... head**: If my eyes are reliable

We were awaked; straightway, at liberty –   235
Where we, in all our trim, freshly beheld
Our royal, good, and gallant ship – our Master
Cap'ring to eye her. On a trice, so please you,
Even in a dream, were we divided from them,
And were brought moping hither.

ARIEL   (*Aside to* PROSPERO) Was't well done?   240

PROSPERO   (*Aside to* ARIEL) Bravely, my diligence. Thou shalt be
            free.

ALONSO   This is as strange a maze as e'er men trod;
          And there is in this business more than nature
          Was ever conduct of. Some oracle
          Must rectify our knowledge!

PROSPERO   Sir, my liege,   245
          Do not infest your mind with beating on
          The strangeness of this business. At picked leisure
          Which shall be shortly single, I'll resolve you –
          Which to you shall seem probable – of every
          These happened accidents. Till when, be cheerful,   250
          And think of each thing well. (*Aside to* ARIEL) Come
            hither, Spirit.
          Set Caliban and his companions free.
          Untie the spell.

                              Exit ARIEL.

          (*To* ALONSO) How fares my gracious sir?
          There are yet missing of your company
          Some few odd lads that you remember not.   255

Re-enter ARIEL, *driving* CALIBAN – *with* STEPHANO *and* TRINCULO
(in their stolen clothes) – ahead of him.

STEPHANO Every man shift for all the rest, and let no man take care
          for himself: for all is but fortune. Coragio, bully-
          monster, coragio!

TRINCULO If these be true spies which I wear in my head, here's a
          goodly sight!   260

Alonso recognizes Stephano and Trinculo as his servants, and Prospero accepts that he is responsible for Caliban.

261 **Setebos**: the god of Sycorax, Caliban's mother

263 **chastise**: punish

266 **Is a plain**: is plainly a

267 **badges**: 1 worn to show which lord they serve; or 2 outward appearances (and the stolen garments)

268 **true**: honest

270 **make … ebbs**: control the tides

271 **deal … power**: i.e. even though less powerful than the moon, she could take over its control

Think about

- Antonio's comment on Caliban in lines 265 to 266 is the only thing he says between meeting Prospero and the end of the play. How would you direct the actor playing the role to behave? Think about whether he should appear repentant, for example.

- What different meanings might there be in Prospero's statement about Caliban, 'This thing of darkness I Acknowledge mine' (lines 275 to 276)?

278 **had he**: did he get

279 **reeling ripe**: so drunk that he is staggering

280 **gilded 'em**: made their faces red

283–4 **fly-blowing**: being infested by maggots, i.e. Trinculo will never become rotten flesh, as he has been well 'pickled'

287 **sirrah**: a term used to an inferior

288 **sore**: 1 in pain; 2 harsh

CALIBAN	O Setebos, these be brave spirits indeed! How fine my master is! I am afraid He will chastise me.
SEBASTIAN	Ha, ha! What things are these, my lord Antonio? Will money buy 'em?

ANTONIO   Very like. One of them   265
Is a plain fish, and, no doubt, marketable.

PROSPERO Mark but the badges of these men, my lords –
Then say if they be true. This mis-shapen knave,
His mother was a witch – and one so strong
That could control the moon, make flows and ebbs,   270
And deal in her command, without her power.
These three have robbed me; and this demi-devil –
For he's a bastard one – had plotted with them
To take my life. Two of these fellows *you*
Must know and own. This thing of darkness I   275
Acknowledge mine.

CALIBAN   I shall be pinched to death.

ALONSO Is not this Stephano, my drunken butler?

SEBASTIAN He is drunk now. Where had he wine?

ALONSO And Trinculo is reeling ripe. Where should they
Find this grand liquor that hath gilded 'em?   280
How cam'st thou in this pickle?

TRINCULO I have been in such a pickle, since I saw you last, that,
I fear me, will never out of my bones. I shall not fear fly-
blowing.

SEBASTIAN Why, how now, Stephano!   285

STEPHANO O, touch me not! I am not Stephano, but a cramp.

PROSPERO You'd be King o'the isle, sirrah?

STEPHANO I should have been a sore one, then.

ALONSO (*Pointing to* CALIBAN) This is a strange thing as e'er I
      looked on.

Prospero invites Alonso and his companions to rest in his cave, promising to take them to their ship in the morning. Finally, he sets Ariel free.

Think about

- What do you think Prospero means by 'Every third thought shall be my grave' (line 311)?

- What do you think Caliban's final words about 'seeking for grace' mean (in lines 294 to 295) and how sincere do you think he is? How would you show him at the end of the play – repentant or still resentful and defiant? What will become of him?

292 **as you look**: if you hope
293 **trim**: tidy

295 **seek for grace**: hope to receive forgiveness / goodwill

298 **luggage**: i.e. the stolen clothes

302 **waste**: pass away the time
303 **discourse**: conversation

305 **accidents gone by**: incidents that have happened

308 **nuptial**: wedding
309 **solemnized**: i.e. made official in a church

313 **Take**: captivate
     deliver: report

314 **auspicious gales**: favourable winds
315 **sail so expeditious**: such a swift voyage
     catch: catch up with
317 **charge**: job

PROSPERO	He is as disproportioned in his manners	290
	As in his shape. Go, sirrah, to my cell:	
	Take with you your companions. As you look	
	To have my pardon, trim it handsomely.	
CALIBAN	Ay, that I will. And I'll be wise hereafter,	
	And seek for grace. What a thrice-double ass	295
	Was I, to take this drunkard for a god,	
	And worship this dull fool!	
PROSPERO	Go to: away!	
ALONSO	Hence, and bestow your luggage where you found it.	
SEBASTIAN	Or stole it, rather.	

Exit CALIBAN, *with* STEPHANO *and* TRINCULO.

PROSPERO	Sir, I invite your Highness and your train	300
	To my poor cell, where you shall take your rest	
	For this one night – which, part of it, I'll waste	
	With such discourse as, I not doubt, shall make it	
	Go quick away: the story of my life,	
	And the particular accidents gone by	305
	Since I came to this isle. And in the morn	
	I'll bring you to your ship, and so to Naples,	
	Where I have hope to see the nuptial	
	Of these our dear-belovèd solemnized;	
	And thence retire me to my Milan, where	310
	Every third thought shall be my grave.	
ALONSO	I long	
	To hear the story of your life, which must	
	Take the ear strangely.	
PROSPERO	I'll deliver all –	
	And promise you calm seas, auspicious gales,	
	And sail so expeditious, that shall catch	315
	Your royal fleet far off. (*To* ARIEL) My Ariel, chick,	
	That is thy charge. Then to the elements	
	Be free, and fare thou well! (*To* ALONSO) Please you,	
	draw near.	

Exit ARIEL. ALONSO *and the others move away towards*
Prospero's cave. Only PROSPERO *remains.*

Prospero asks the audience to release him from the island by applauding the play.

1 **charms ... o'erthrown**: spells broken

7 **the deceiver**: i.e. Antonio

9 **bands**: bonds
10 **hands**: i.e. the audience's applause
11 **Gentle breath**: 1 a favourable breeze; 2 approval or cheers (from the audience)
13 **want**: lack
14 **enforce**: control
Art: magic power
16 **prayer**: his plea 1 to the audience; 2 to God for his mercy
17 **pierces**: gets through and is accepted
17–18 **assaults ... itself**: penetrates the heart of mercy
18 **frees all faults**: allows all sins to be forgiven
19 **would pardoned be**: would want to be pardoned
20 **indulgence**: favour / goodwill

___Think about___

• Which parts of this final speech can be read as applying to both Prospero on his island, and the actor on his stage?

• Some actors deliver this speech in the character of Prospero, while others come out of the part and speak in their own identity as actors. Which would you choose if you were performing the role? Think about what effect you would want to achieve.

Spoken by PROSPERO *(to the audience).*

Now my charms are all o'erthrown,
And what strength I have's mine own –
Which is most faint. Now 'tis true
I must be here confined by you,
Or sent to Naples. Let me not,   5
Since I have my dukedom got
And pardoned the deceiver, dwell
In this bare island by your spell;
But release me from my bands
With the help of your good hands.   10
Gentle breath of yours my sails
Must fill, or else my project fails –
Which was to please. Now I want
Spirits to enforce, Art to enchant;
And my ending is despair,   15
Unless I be relieved by prayer,
Which pierces so that it assaults
Mercy itself and frees all faults.
   As you from crimes would pardoned be,
   Let your indulgence set me free.   20

Exit.

RSC, 1998

RSC, 1993

RSC, 1982

RSC, 1998

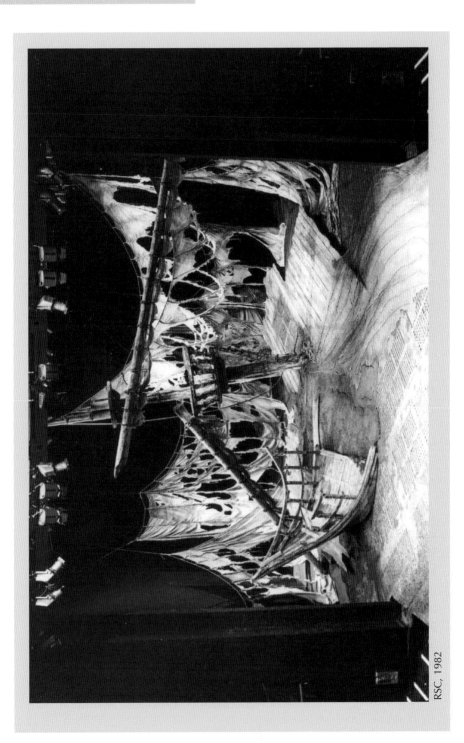

RSC, 1982

RSC, 1993

The Tempest was written around 1611, a time when European countries had only just begun to 'discover' many parts of the world. The effects of this can be seen throughout *The Tempest*.

TRAVELLERS' TALES

At the time Shakespeare was writing, explorers and travellers were returning to England with wild and strange stories. Many were gruesome, telling of men with two heads or lands that were inhabited by devils. Others were exotic and fantastical, telling of men with magic powers like ancient gods or men who could fly. The island in *The Tempest* seems to reflect the range of these stories. It can seem to be a paradise or a hell depending on who is observing it:

ADRIAN   The air breathes upon us here most sweetly.
SEBASTIAN   As if it had lungs, and rotten ones.

COLONISING THE 'NEW WORLD'

When Europeans sailed to lands that were new to them, they would often claim the territories as their own despite the fact that they were already inhabited. These lands would then become colonies, ruled by the Europeans. Many European colonists thought of the native peoples as little better than animals – creatures with no language. They believed they had the right to conquer the native peoples and force them to accept European ideas. In the early American colonies the native Americans helped the colonists survive through the first harsh winters. But they soon began to dislike being dominated and treated badly by the settlers and started to fight for their freedom.

All this can be seen in the story of Caliban. He claims that the island is his, and that he helped Prospero and Miranda to find food and water when they first arrived. To begin with, Prospero and Miranda taught Caliban how to use language and treated him well. However, after attempting to rape Miranda, Caliban became their slave in a place where he was once the only king. This is why Prospero's treatment of Caliban is often seen as a picture of the way Europeans colonised other peoples – conquering them, taking their countries' riches and making their men, women and children into slaves.

MAGIC AND THE SUPERNATURAL

In Shakespeare's England many people believed in witches, devils and the power of magic. Education was limited and science had not yet established itself as a system for explaining unusual phenomena. As a result people were inclined to believe that things they could not explain had to be supernatural. For example, the work of Dr John Dee, a famous Elizabethan mathematician and geographer, was genuinely scientific but he was also an astrologer and regarded as a magician.

In *The Tempest*, Prospero's magic is a mixture of the scientific (he learned his 'art' through study) and the supernatural (he has immense powers over nature). He can control the elements, dim the sun, and make graves open and give up their dead. However, behind these powers there is a logic and a reasoning/scientific mind. He uses his powers to enforce a kind of justice and to punish those who are guilty until they repent and are worthy of forgiveness. Indeed, once his plans are complete he renounces his magic and it is clear that the supernatural has its limitations and is not a substitute for genuine human relationships.

ROMANCES

Four of Shakespeare's final plays (*Pericles*, *Cymbeline*, *The Winter's Tale* and *The Tempest*) are sometimes called the 'romances'. A romance today would simply be a love story. In Shakespeare's time a romance was an adventure-story set in an exotic place or places, which included strange events, larger-than-life characters and elements of magic or the supernatural.
The Tempest, with its island peopled by a magician and his daughter, a spirit and a monster, contains all of these ingredients.

These activities focus on different scenes in the play. The type of activities used can easily be adapted to focus on other sections of the play if necessary. Before beginning the activities you will need to have read the relevant scene, unless otherwise stated.

Act 1 Scene 1: the shipwreck

Each activity in this section leads directly on to the next. The focus of the activities is on the action of the scene and the effect of the storm on the audience. The major activity is in two parts, 'Preparing the scene' and 'Playing the scene'. However, 'Preparing the scene' can be undertaken as an activity in its own right and is a useful way of taking the scene apart to look at its structure.

Preparing the scene

The staging of the first scene is very important. If the audience is not convinced that the shipwreck seems real then they will not be amazed when they discover that the storm came from Prospero's magic and that everyone is safe. Despite the sense of panic in Act 1 Scene 1, there is a strong structure to the scene. It is through this that many important themes and relationships are established.

1   Divide into 3 groups:

- Group A: the passengers
- Group B: the Boatswain and crew on deck
- Group C: the crew elsewhere on ship

Group A

a   Read the scene noting down the lines that you consider most important. From these write a shortened version of the scene. You must keep in all the instructions the Boatswain issues to his men, and all the lines spoken by the crew.

b   Cast the following characters from your group: Alonso, Ferdinand, Gonzalo, Sebastian, Antonio. Other members of Group A should be attendants to King Alonso.

GROUP B

a Through the scene the Boatswain is trying to keep the ship in open water, away from rocks that are likely to be close to shore. Go through the scene and write out a list of all the instructions the Boatswain gives to his men.

Example

Take in the topsail.

b Using these lines make up a scene showing what the sailors on deck are doing during Act 1 Scene 1. Put in as much action as possible, remembering the urgency and panic. One member of the group should be the Boatswain, one should be the ship's Master and the rest of the group should be sailors.

Example

Half the sailors might be following the Boatswain's instructions, taking in the topsail, etc. Others might be trying to bail out the water that is coming into the ship.

GROUP C

a Write a scene to show what the crew below deck are doing during Act 1 Scene 1. This should be in 3 parts:

- Part 1, lines 1 to 33: Think of some ideas for activities being carried out below deck. For example, the mariners could be parcelling up any remaining food and provisions.

- Part 2, lines 33 to 56: Imagine that the cry heard from below happens when the water reaches the hold for the first time and that this is why the crew who appear on deck soon afterwards are wet. Improvise a dialogue to show the panic and distress when this happens.

- Part 3, lines 57 to 59: These lines are spoken by the crew when they realise the ship is splitting apart and that they will drown. Each person in the group should think of a series of lines for this section of the scene. You can use the lines from the text as well as lines of your own.

Example

'Farewell my wife and children, for I shall never see you again.'

PLAYING THE SCENE

1 a Group A should read out the scene that they wrote in the previous task with Group B reading the Boatswain's and crew's lines. The others should try to imagine the action as clearly as they can.

b Group A should act out their scene. From line 25 onwards the people playing Alonso and Ferdinand should go and pray below deck – you can say the Lord's Prayer or any that you know.

Group B should add in the actions and dialogue for the Boatswain and sailors on deck.

Group C should add in the action for the crew from below deck. The actors speaking the lines scripted by Group A must try to get on top of all other noise.

c Act the scene through one more time. This time you should play it at twice the speed to highlight the urgency and panic.

LOOKING AT THE SCENE

1 In pairs, list three important moments in the scene for:
- Alonso and his companions
- the Master, Boatswain and the sailors on deck
- the crew below deck.

2 In pairs imagine that you are directing this scene. Decide:
- Who do you think has most control and authority in this scene, the King and nobles, or the ship's Master and Boatswain?
- How would you make this clear to the audience?

ACT 1 SCENE 2: PROSPERO AND THE PLAN

Each activity in this section leads directly on to the next. However, it is possible to use any of them separately. You only need to have read the scene summary on page 32 before beginning these activities. The focus of the activities is on the methods Prospero uses to set his plan in motion.

THE PAST

Prospero tells Miranda that the time has come for her to be told about their past. He tells her that he was the Duke of Milan, but allowed his brother, Antonio, to govern the state while he devoted himself to academic study. This awakened an evil nature in his brother – Antonio wanted to overthrow Prospero and become Duke in his own right.

1 **a** In pairs read lines 120 to 168 where Prospero tells the story of the midnight capture of him and Miranda by Antonio's men and the men of the King of Naples.

  b Write a film script of this dramatic account. You should write a voice-over telling the story as a flashback account of the action. Then write the action or visuals that would appear on screen in brackets alongside your script.
  Example
  'The clock struck midnight. All was silent in the palace. Suddenly a door burst open …'
  (The camera pans around the dimly lit but expensively furnished palace.)

  You should focus on the most dramatic moments, for example, Prospero finding that the boat in which they have been put to sea is very weak and about to sink, or the moment when they find the provisions that Gonzalo has stored away for them.

2 **a** In groups of six to eight, choose one of the film scripts that you have written. Decide who will play each of the characters you need to act out the scene. You will also need to choose one person to be the older Miranda listening to the story and one person to be Prospero, speaking the voice-over.

  b Act out the film script with the older Miranda watching the action and listening to the narrator.

c   In the play both the audience and Miranda are hearing the story for the first time. Because of this, in most productions, the audience identify strongly with Miranda. In your group take it in turns to ask the person playing the older Miranda questions about the events she has just watched. For example, you could ask her about her feelings towards the people who cast her and her father out of Milan.

3 a   Hearing this 'story' means that the audience are likely to have an opinion about key characters in the play before they see them on the island. In groups or as a class choose three people to take the roles of Alonso, Antonio, and Gonzalo. The rest of the group is the 'audience'.

b   The 'audience' should question these characters about why they acted as they did all those years ago.
Examples
'Gonzalo – how did you know what to provide for Prospero and Miranda?'
'Alonso – how did Antonio persuade you to help to overthrow a lawful ruler?'

c   As a group discuss how the audience feel about each of the characters after they have heard this story. Does this fit in with the way we have seen the three characters behave during the shipwreck in Act 1 Scene 1?

PROSPERO AND ARIEL

Magic is central to both the theme and the plot of *The Tempest*. From Prospero's conversations with Miranda and Ariel we learn that the storm was 'performed' by Ariel and only appeared to destroy the ship and crew. In order for Prospero's magic to have its intended effect, it is vital that the characters in the play believe in Prospero's illusions, such as the storm.

1   Read through Ariel's account of the storm in lines 195 to 215. Imagine that you are Ferdinand. Write a journal entry about the dreadful storm and the events right up to the moment when you decide to jump overboard. In it you should describe what you can see and how you are feeling.

2   In pairs discuss the image that you have of Prospero at the end of this scene. How strong do you think his magic is?

THE CONTRAST BETWEEN CALIBAN AND FERDINAND

Part of Prospero's plan is that Miranda should fall in love with Prince Ferdinand. Miranda comes straight from Caliban when she meets Ferdinand for the first time, which makes the contrast between them as strong as possible – perhaps this is what Prospero intended.

1 When Caliban enters (at line 322) he is spitting curses on Prospero and Miranda. For example, 'A south-west blow on ye and blister you all o'er!' (lines 324 to 325).

   a In pairs find the rest of the curses Caliban uses from line 322 to 366.

   b With your partner make up and write down five curses that Caliban might use on Prospero and Miranda.

   c As a group pick out the best of these.

   d As a group discuss why it seems right for Caliban's character to be spitting curses. In a play where magic is a central element, do we ever imagine that these curses might come true?

2 Prospero mentions Caliban's attempted rape of Miranda (lines 348 to 349). He might want this to be in her mind when she meets Ferdinand to highlight how his behaviour differs from Caliban's. Imagine that you are Miranda thinking back to this experience. Answer the following questions:

   • How long ago was the incident?
   • Where did the incident take place?
   • How frightened were you at the time?
   • Did Prospero stop Caliban? How?
   • How did you feel immediately afterwards?
   • How did the incident change the way you felt towards Caliban?

3 a In pairs one of you should take the part of Ferdinand and the other should be Miranda. The person playing Ferdinand should pretend to be alone, wandering on the island. The person playing Miranda should follow him secretly and make comments about everything wonderful that she notices about him.
Example
Look at his eyes! Such beautiful soulful eyes!

b Work out an action for the moment when Ferdinand first sees Miranda. Try to create the feeling that a spell has been cast. Prospero says: 'At the first sight they have changed eyes' (lines 444 to 445).
Example
Perhaps Ferdinand and Miranda could both gasp and then bow or curtsey because they believe that the person they see before them must be a god or goddess.

ACT 2 SCENE 1: THE GOOD AND THE BAD

Each activity in this section leads directly on to the next. However, it is possible to use any of them separately. The focus of the activities is on the difference between the motivation and intent of Gonzalo and Alonso, compared with Antonio and Sebastian.

THE GOOD

This scene separates the characters with good intentions (Gonzalo and Alonso) from the villains (Sebastian and Antonio).

1   Gonzalo is struck with the joy of being alive and with wonder at what he sees as a fertile green island. He spends most of the scene attempting to comfort Alonso who is filled with grief because he believes that his son, Ferdinand, is dead.

   a   In pairs read lines 1 to 177, listing all the reasons that Gonzalo gives for his companions to be happy or thankful.
   Examples
   'Our escape is much beyond our loss.' (lines 2 to 3)
   'But for the miracle, I mean our preservation.' (lines 6 to 7)

   b   Write these key lines up into a speech in modern language.
   Example
   Your majesty, being saved is a miracle itself! We should think of our escape and not make ourselves depressed by concentrating on what we have lost.

   c   Alonso, however, is beyond comfort. This is important because it reveals how deep his love for his son is. One of you should now take the role of Alonso and the other should be Gonzalo. Gonzalo reads out the speech you have written, pausing for Alonso to speak his thoughts after each sentence.
   Example
   Gonzalo: We should think of our escape and not dwell on what we have lost.
   Alonso's thought: You can say that, old man, because you have not lost your children. I will never see Claribel again and Ferdinand is drowned.

2 **a** Gonzalo's speech (lines 143 to 152) describes how he would organise things if he were king of the island. In pairs decide whether you think the following conditions would be good or bad in a state. Copy down the list and next to each item write either 'good', 'bad' or 'can't decide'.

- No trade
- No legal system
- No education
- No rich and poor
- No servants
- No inherited land (land passing from parent to child)
- No jobs
- No king

b Discuss whether such a place could exist. Do you think that nature left to its own devices would be positive or negative? For example, think about what has shaped the character of Caliban.

3 At line 177 Ariel enters playing solemn music that sends everyone except Sebastian and Antonio to sleep.

a In pairs write a description of the dreams that Gonzalo and Alonso might have while they are asleep. For example, Gonzalo might dream of his commonwealth; Alonso might dream about finding Ferdinand, either dead or alive.

b Discuss what the dreams you have imagined might show about the characters and their states of mind at this moment in the play.

THE MAGIC ISLAND – GOOD OR BAD?

The island is seen quite differently by the 'good' and 'bad' characters. For example, for Gonzalo it is a lush, green paradise, but for Sebastian and Antonio it is a dark, unpleasant place.

1 **a** In pairs read lines 35 to 62 and note down the different ways the characters see the island.

b One of you should be Gonzalo and the other should be Antonio. Imagine that you are both on a hilltop looking out over the island. Take it in turns to describe what you can hear, see and smell.

c Discuss why you think the two characters see the island so differently. What do you think this reveals about the characters of Gonzalo and Antonio?

THE VILLAINS

In this scene Antonio and Sebastian show what they are really like. First, they mock Gonzalo's attempts to cheer Alonso up and harshly criticise Alonso for giving his daughter in marriage to the King of Tunis. Then, when they have promised to protect Alonso whilst the others sleep, they plot to murder him instead.

1 a In pairs read lines 192 to 288. In this section Antonio persuades Sebastian that they should kill Alonso. Make a list of the arguments he uses.
   Example
   Sebastian is now heir to Naples because Ferdinand is dead and Claribel is out of reach.

   b Improvise the persuasion scene with one of you playing Antonio and the other Sebastian. Antonio should use the arguments which you have listed.

   c Discuss which arguments have the most effect in persuading Sebastian.

   d With your partner answer the following questions:

   • Do you think Ariel's magic has an effect on Antonio and Sebastian as well as on the sleepers? Does the magic, for example, make them reveal their innermost desires?
   • Why does Sebastian say 'O, but one word' (line 288) as they prepare to draw their swords? Do you think he is having second thoughts or does he want to change the plan in some way?
   • Does Sebastian's momentary pause at this point make us see his character any differently?

2 In pairs discuss your impressions so far of the character of Antonio. How would you describe him as:

• a man?
• a ruler?
• a brother?

ACT 2 SCENE 2: THE CLOWNS

Each activity in this section leads directly on to the next. However, it is possible to use any of them separately. The focus of the activities is on the nature and function of comedy in *The Tempest*.

In productions of the play Act 2 Scene 2 is one of the high points because it has lots of visual humour and a spirit of carnival. The scene introduces us to the comic characters Trinculo and Stephano, and allows us to see a different side of the character of Caliban.

CALIBAN

The more bitter and angry Caliban is in the opening speech (lines 1 to 14), the more comical it is when he becomes submissive later on in the scene. Many directors ask the actor playing Caliban to 'feel' the pain of unseen pinches throughout this speech. Caliban's reactions to these pinches set up the physical and visual nature of this scene.

1   a   In pairs go through the speech and find three places where it would make sense for Caliban to feel a sudden stab of pain.

   b   One person should then read the speech whilst in the role of Caliban gathering wood. The other person should clap when they want Caliban to feel a jolt of pain. Caliban must react to the pain and with each jolt become more angry. Try to build in as many physical actions as possible, for example, the pain could cause Caliban to drop the logs – he could even drop them on to his toe to add to his pain.

2   a   Caliban is always a popular character with actors because there are many different sides of his character. In this scene, for example, he goes from bitterly cursing Prospero to worshipping Stephano with drunken child-like enthusiasm. In pairs read through the scene and make a list of all the adjectives you would use to describe Caliban.

   b   In some productions Caliban is played as a monster, both in appearance and personality. In others he is more of a curiosity. Consider:

   • If you were the director how much of a monster would you want Caliban to be?
   • How would your costume for the character reflect this?
   • Which of the Calibans shown in the photographs on pages 12 and 13 come closest to your vision of the character? Why?

SLAPSTICK COMEDY

1 The comedy between Trinculo, Stephano, and Caliban includes a lot
of slapstick – it is physical and depends on action and reactions as
much as on words. Below is a list of what happens in the section in
which the three characters discover each other. In groups of three use
the list to create a scene in the style of a silent movie. Make each
gesture as big as you can and make sure each 'reaction' is aimed
straight out at the audience. You can use sounds but no words.

- Caliban is cursing Prospero.
- Caliban hears someone coming. He thinks it is a spirit and falls flat
  on the ground under his cloak, hoping not to be seen.
- Trinculo enters. He spots Caliban and goes to investigate, first
  reacting to his strong fish-like smell.
- Holding his nose, Trinculo checks the parts of Caliban he can see
  trying to work out what he is, and whether he is dead or alive.
- Hearing more thunder, Trinculo decides to keep dry under
  Caliban's cloak and crawls in.
- Stephano, who is already drunk, enters with his bottle of strong
  wine.
- Caliban, perhaps being tickled under the cloak by Trinculo, calls
  out in fear of the 'spirit'.
- Stephano sees Caliban/Trinculo and thinks that he is a monster
  with four legs.
- Stephano pours drink into Caliban's mouth – Caliban loves it.
- Trinculo calls out – Stephano, thinking it is a monster with two
  heads and two voices, backs away, terrified.
- Trinculo calls out again and Stephano recognises his voice.
- Stephano begins, with great difficulty, to pull Trinculo out from
  under the cloak – the more Stephano heaves, the more Caliban is
  tickled.

STATUS AND BUSINESS

The comedy in the last part of the scene mainly comes from Caliban worshipping Stephano and his 'celestial liquor', and from all three of them wanting to drink as much of this strong wine as possible.

1 In groups of three as the characters of Caliban, Stephano, and Trinculo:

   a Act out lines 137 to 144 with each character trying to get the bottle. For example, Trinculo could be trying to grab the bottle back from Caliban, who is very reluctant to give it up, through his whole speech (lines 139 to 142).

   b Act out lines 143 to 171. Each time Caliban declares that he will worship, love, or help Stephano, he must make a grand gesture of being completely humble. For example, he could throw himself to the ground or be trying desperately to kiss Stephano's feet. With every gesture Caliban makes, Stephano should act more and more like a king.

2 a Discuss the atmosphere of the scene, which seems to be summed up by Caliban's last speech (lines 174 to 181). Remember that the scenes with Caliban, Stephano, and Trinculo are the only action on the island that is not part of Prospero's plan. Consider:

   • What might the audience be thinking and feeling at the end of the scene?
   • What is it about the characters of Trinculo and Stephano that audiences enjoy most?
   • Might the audience believe that these three characters are capable of disrupting Prospero's plan?

   b In this scene, we have seen different aspects of Caliban. Make lists of:

   • Caliban's faults and weaknesses
   • Caliban's good or positive qualities.

   c From what you know about Caliban at this point in the play, decide what would make a happy ending for this character.

ACT 3 SCENE 1: THE LOVERS

Each activity in this section leads directly on to the next. However, it is possible to use any of them separately. The focus of the activities is on the relationship of Ferdinand and Miranda and its importance for the future.

1 a In pairs read through Act 3 Scene 1 and write a shortened version of the scene. Ferdinand and Miranda should speak about 10 lines each. These can be lines selected from the text or lines that you have written yourself.

  b If Ferdinand had been introduced to a prospective bride in Naples, he would have had to follow strict rules about how to woo her. However, Miranda's openness and simplicity force him to abandon much of the etiquette of courtship. Even so Miranda speaks more directly than Ferdinand.

MIRANDA   Do you love me?

FERDINAND   O heaven, O earth, bear witness to this sound
               And crown what I profess with kind event,
               If I speak true! If hollowly, invert
               What best is boded me to mischief! I,
               Beyond all limit of what else i'the world,
               Do love, prize, honour you.

Perhaps if Ferdinand had asked the question, Miranda's answer would have been a simple yes. In pairs go through the scene and find other examples of this difference in the way they think and speak.

  c Read the shortened version you wrote in part **a**. Does your version reflect this? Make any changes to your scene that you think are necessary to show this different way in which they think and speak.

d The log-bearing task makes this scene much less awkward than some first love scenes. It also means that some formalities are abandoned. For example, Ferdinand cannot bow to Miranda when he sees her, or kiss her hand, because he is carrying a heavy load.

The log-bearing also gives the scene a game-like quality. Make a stack of logs (for example, rolled up newspapers) and place them to one side of a small space you have cleared to act out the scene. In pairs, one of you playing Ferdinand and the other Miranda, act out your shortened version of the scene whilst trying to:

- carry as many logs as you can to the other side of the room
- stop the other person from carrying logs, taking the logs from them if necessary.

e The log-bearing also means that Miranda and Ferdinand are likely to make physical contact. It is very hard to take logs from another person without brushing their fingers or touching their arm. Decide with your partner where you think the first moment of physical contact should come. Make a freeze-frame of this moment. With your partner decide what each of the characters is thinking and feeling at this point.

f In a production the words in this scene could be less important than the moments of contact, eye contact, the smiles and even the silences between the characters. Go through your shortened version of the scene again and experiment with putting in silences where both characters are simply happy to work alongside each other carrying logs. Decide where such periods of silence might work best.

2 In pairs discuss the way the audience feel towards Miranda and Ferdinand at the end of the scene. The optimistic ending of the play largely depends on the audience trusting in the relationship of Miranda and Ferdinand. What is it that makes us confident that the relationship will grow and last?

PROSPERO THE SILENT OBSERVER

Prospero's plan is working. By putting obstacles in the way of the relationship he has made Ferdinand and Miranda love each other more. It is essential that their love is deep and real. At the end of the play, Prospero will be able to give up his magic only if there is a new and lasting power for good that will replace it – the power of love. Love will also be the means by which old divisions will be overcome and old sins wiped out. Miranda and Ferdinand must be King and Queen jointly ruling Naples and Milan.

1 **a** Read Prospero's speech at the end of the scene, lines 92 to 96.

   b Imagine you are Prospero at the end of this scene. Complete the following sentences:

   - I think …
   - I feel …
   - I want …

2 Imagine that you are Prospero once he has left the island, describing the events which happened in this scene to a friend in Milan. Tell the story of it from Prospero's viewpoint, remembering that he was a silent observer but was also deeply involved in what was happening. As Prospero you might consider the following:

   - How do you feel when you see the moments of physical contact between Miranda and Ferdinand?
   - Are you surprised at how outspoken Miranda is about her feelings?
   - Why are you convinced that this young man will do a good job of looking after your daughter?

ACT 5 SCENE 1: A BRAVE NEW WORLD

Each activity in this section leads directly on to the next. However, it is possible to use any of them separately. The focus of the activities is on the new order that is established.

The key effect of Prospero's magic is that it sets in motion the process of renewal and regeneration of the characters who have sinned in the past. Prospero takes on a god-like role and the sinners are punished and then forgiven. In the last scene of the play, the characters find each other. More importantly, they find themselves, or become the people they have the potential to be. This is the brave new world that Miranda enters into when she sees these handsome creatures. For others, however, especially Antonio, this brave new world holds little or no attraction.

THE RESTORATION OF SANITY

At the end of Act 3 Ariel appeared like a Harpy and drove Alonso, Antonio and Sebastian mad by reminding them of their sins. At the beginning of Act 5 Ariel reports to Prospero on their condition.

1   a   Read through Ariel's speech (lines 7 to 19).

    b   Gonzalo has gone from joy and wonder at the island to fear and sorrow at the suffering of King Alonso and the others. Imagine that you are Gonzalo. Make up a speech in which you describe the awful things that have happened to the three men. Consider:

- How is the madness showing itself – what signs can you see?
- Are they all behaving the same or is the madness affecting them differently?
- Do you think they will ever recover their senses?

2   Prospero dissolves the charm that is working on the men and, dressed again as the Duke of Milan, welcomes them to the island (from line 106). The moment in which the lords recognise Prospero is important.

    a   As a group model a freeze-frame of this moment using the characters of Prospero, Alonso, Sebastian, Antonio, and Gonzalo.

    b   Discuss what might be going through the minds of King Alonso and his companions.

3 a Read lines 106 to 215 to trace the inner 'journeys' of Alonso, Gonzalo, Sebastian and Antonio. Consider what each of the four characters is thinking during these lines.

b In pairs first make a list of each piece of information that is revealed to the men. Next write the thought-line for each of the four characters in reaction to the news.
Example
Information: Prospero is alive.
Alonso: Surely this is Prospero, Duke of Milan.
Antonio: What trick is this! Prospero was left for dead!

4 a Alonso is obviously sorry and wants forgiveness. How far do you think Antonio and Sebastian have been cleansed of their faults? Consider the following questions:

- Why do they hardly speak through this section of the scene? (Antonio, in fact, speaks only once before the end of the play, which is to comment on Caliban.)
- Why does Prospero let them know that he might at some later time reveal that they had planned to kill Alonso?

b As a group model a freeze-frame of the characters' positions at line 215, when Gonzalo says 'Be it so! Amen!' Decide what Sebastian and Antonio might be feeling at this time.

PROSPERO'S JOURNEY

1 a Read through lines 17 to 32. In productions this sequence between Prospero and Ariel is often one of the most moving scenes in the play. Getting revenge on those who betrayed him would be easy for Prospero. How easy is it for him, do you think, to forgive and release them?

b Imagine that you are Prospero after Ariel's exit at line 32. Complete the following sentences:

- I feel …
- I want …
- I hope …

2 In a powerful speech Prospero tells the audience that once he has restored the sanity of the lords, he will break his staff and drown his magic book.

   a In pairs read lines 33 to 57 out loud. One person should read until the first full stop or semi-colon. The second person should then take over until the next full stop or semi-colon and so on through the speech. Each time you change readers, the person taking over must speak more loudly and strongly, so that the speech builds in intensity.

   b The speech is full of vivid images. With your partner list these and describe each one in as much detail as possible.
   Example
   'Ye elves of hills, brooks, standing lakes, and groves'
   Decide what these elves look like, how many there might be, etc.

   c Discuss the effect of this speech on the audience. For example, do you think that it might change the way the audience feels about the character of Prospero?

   d Prospero intends to return to Milan as a man rather than as a magician. Do you think that without his magic he will be a good ruler? Make a list of the qualities he possesses that will help him to keep a peaceful state. Consider the following questions:

   • What do we know have been Prospero's shortcomings as a ruler in the past?
   • What do you think he has learned since last being Duke of Milan?
   • Do you think that when Prospero forgives the nobles he also forgives himself for neglecting his duties when he was Duke of Milan?

THE FUTURE – A BRAVE NEW WORLD?

Miranda's openness and joy at seeing the collection of lords, 'O brave new world, that has such people in't!' (lines 183 to 184) affects the atmosphere of the play as it comes to an end. The characters have found each other and many, having been forgiven for their sins, have found themselves. It is a kind of freedom – freedom from guilt.

Ariel too has been freed, and even Caliban intends to be wiser and seek grace. Prospero's magic has rewritten the past and set up the future. After the end of the play, Prospero will tell them all the story of his life on the island, then they will travel back to Naples for the marriage of Ferdinand and Miranda.

1 Imagine that you are Prospero at the banquet after the end of the play. You have promised to tell Alonso everything. Will you? Write an account of the story you would tell. Consider the following questions:

   • Will you tell the story of Caliban's attempted rape of Miranda?
   • Will you tell Alonso about Antonio and Sebastian's plot or will you keep this back as something you can reveal in the future, if you need to?

2 Imagine that you are a courtier at the court of Naples. Your king has returned with his son and also with Prospero and Miranda who you believed had been lost many years ago. Write an eye-witness account of Prospero's reception by the courtiers of Naples, and of the marriage of Ferdinand and Miranda.